Book 3

Just Grammar

Intermediate

Includes
Answer Key

Jeremy Harmer
with Hester Lott

Viva Books

New Delhi | Mumbai | Chennai | Kolkata | Bangalore | Hyderabad | Kochi | Guwahati

Photo acknowledgements
Corbis: pages 36, 37, 42, 61, 64, 79;
Getty images: pages 25, 33, 53.

First Indian Edition 2009

VIVA BOOKS PRIVATE LIMITED

- 4737/23 Ansari Road, Daryaganj, New Delhi 110 002
  E-mail: vivadelhi@vivagroupindia.net, Tel. 42242200
- 76, Service Industries, Shirvane, Sector 1, Nerul, Navi Mumbai 400 706
  E-mail: vivamumbai@vivagroupindia.net, Tel. 27721273, 27721274
- Jamals Fazal Chambers, 26 Greams Road, Chennai 600 006
  E-mail: vivachennai@vivagroupindia.net, Tel. 28290304, 28294241
- B-103, Jindal Towers, 21/1A/3 Darga Road, Kolkata 700 017
  E-mail: vivakolkata@vivagroupindia.net, Tel. 22836381, 22816713
- 7, Sovereign Park Apartments, 56-58, K. R. Road, Basavanagudi, Bangalore 560 004
  E-mail: vivabangalore@vivagroupindia.net, Tel. 26607409, 26607410
- 101-102 Mughal Marc Apartments, 3-4-637 to 641, Narayanguda, Hyderabad 500 029
  E-mail: vivahyderabad@vivagroupindia.net, Tel. 27564481, 27564482
- First Floor, Beevi Towers, SRM Road, Kaloor, Kochi 682 018, Kerala
  E-mail: vivakochi@vivagroupindia.net, Tel: 0484-2403055, 2403056
- H. No. 12, P. B. Road, Near Arya Hospital, Rehabari, Guwahati 781 008
  E-mail: vivaguwahati@vivagroupindia.net, Tel: 0361-2735624

www.vivagroupindia.com

Published by arrangement with
Marshall Cavendish Education
119 Wardour Street
London W1F 0UW, UK

ISBN-10: 81-309-1108-6
ISBN-13: 978-81-309-1108-3

Published by Vinod Vasishtha for Viva Books Private Limited, 4737/23, Ansari Road, Daryaganj, New Delhi - 110 002. Printed and bound by Raj Press, R-3, Inderpuri, New Delhi - 110 012.

Contents

Introduction

For the student

Just Grammar (*Intermediate*) is part of an integrated series of books designed for you to study on your own, or together with other students and a teacher. It will help you improve your knowledge and use of English structure. We have carefully chosen the main grammar areas that are important for students at this level.

In this book you will find clear explanations of the grammar you are studying. There are examples to help you understand the explanations too. And then you can do the many exercises in the book which will help you to develop your knowledge and use of English grammar.

When you see this symbol ( ) it means that the answers to the practice exercises are in the answer key at the back of the book. You can check your answers there.

There is an index at the back of the book. This means that you can find words and grammar areas whenever you want.

We are confident that this book will help you progress in English and, above all, that you will enjoy using it.

For the teacher

The *Just* series is a flexible set of teaching materials that can be used on their own, or in any combination, or as a set to form a complete integrated course. The *Just* series has been written and designed using a consistent methodological approach that allows the books to be used easily together. Each book in the series specialises in either language skills or aspects of the English language. It can be used either in class or by students working on their own.

Just Grammar consists of 14 units which offer comprehensive grammar explanations and provide practice activities to improve the student's ability to use the language. Each unit takes one area of grammar (e.g. noun phrases) and then deals with it in three parts. In Part A one aspect of the grammar area is presented (e.g. nouns with adjectives, nouns with prepositional phrases), explained, and practised. Part B presents another aspect of the area (e.g. nouns followed by present and past participles) with more explanations, examples and practice activities. Finally, in Part C, mixed practice of the whole grammar area is offered with more exercises, consisting of contrastive material from Parts A & B.

Students will be able to use *Just Grammar* without needing explanation or guidance on the part of the teacher. Having read through the explanations and examples in the book, they will be able to do the exercises, and then check them in the answer key at the back. However the units are also highly appropriate for work in class.

We have provided an index at the very back of the book to make *Just Grammar* easier to use and access.

We are confident that you will find this book a real asset and we recommend that you also try the other books in the series: *Just Reading and Writing*, *Just Vocabulary* and *Just Listening and Speaking*.

UNIT 1

A The present (1)

present simple • present continuous

1 **Read the following descriptions of the different ways that present tenses can be used.**

present simple

1 We use the present simple to talk about general facts that are true and will be true for some time:

*She **lives** in London.*
*The earth **travels** round the sun.*

2 We use the present simple to talk about repeated actions or habits:

*He **gets up** at six-thirty every morning.*
*I always **cry** during romantic films.*

3 The present simple is often used to tell the stories of films and plays, and in sports commentaries:

*So then he **makes** his way back to Rome and becomes a gladiator.*
*Beckham **passes** the ball to Owen. Owen scores!*

4 Some verbs usually take the present simple rather than the present continuous, whatever the context:

- mental states: ***believe, know, realise, recognise, suppose, think, understand***
- wants and likes: ***want, like, love, hate, need, prefer***
- appearance: ***appear, seem, look like***

*I **know** her very well.* (NOT: ~~*I am knowing her very well.*~~)
*Olivia **seems** rather tired today.* (NOT: ~~*Olivia is seeming rather tired.*~~)

5 The present simple is used to talk about future schedules and arrangements:

*The bus **leaves** at ten o'clock.*
*Her exam **finishes** at two o'clock.*

present continuous

6 We use the present continuous to talk about things that have begun and are not yet finished at the time of speaking:

*They**'re staying** with friends in Italy this week.*
*She**'s watching** the news on television.*

7 We use the present continuous to talk about changes in people and the world around us:

*House prices **are rising**.*
*Keith **is getting** taller every day.*

8 The present continuous is sometimes used with ***always*** to describe repeated actions that occur more often than is expected. This is used in speaking more often than writing.

*He**'s always forgetting** his key.*
*She**'s always complaining** about something.*

9 We use the present continuous to talk about things in the future that we or someone else has arranged:

*I**'m travelling** to Boston next week.*
*She**'s playing** in a concert tomorrow evening.*

Remember: there are certain verbs that do not usually appear in the continuous forms (see 4 opposite).

2 **Choose the correct form (present simple or present continuous) of the verb in brackets and fill the gaps.**

Marek, an artist, (**a** live) .... in London. He (**b** get up) .... at about six o'clock every morning and (**c** drive) .... to work. He (**d** work) .... in a big room because he needs lots of space. At work he (**e** wear) .... old clothes and big gloves. At the moment he (**f** work) .... on a new sculpture for a main square in the city. He (**g** make) .... his sculpture from wood. When he (**h** leave) .... work in the evening, he (**i** drive) .... back home. He has dinner with his family and then he (**j** read) .... to his children before they go to sleep. At the moment they (**k** read) .... a book about a wizard called Harry Potter. When the children are asleep he (**l** watch) .... television with his wife. When he (**m** go) .... to sleep he (**n** dream) .... of wood and metal – and all the sculptures he is going to make one day.

3 **Choose the correct alternative (in blue) in the following sentences. Say which explanation from Exercise 1 fits the verb form you have chosen. The first answer is done for you.**

a ~~We are knowing~~/We know that you did it !

.......explanation 4.......

b Oh, this is dramatic! Peters is running/runs up to the wicket, is bowling/bowls the ball – and it is going/goes right through the batsman's legs. ....

c Hello. What? … I'm on the train … we just leave/are just leaving.

....

d Oh, stop it! You're always telling/You always tell me to tidy my room and it's not fair!

....

e There's no doubt about it. The weather gets/is getting warmer all the time. Global warming is a reality.

....

f When Oscar leaves/is leaving Sidney he is giving/gives a note to Lucinda. He tells/is telling her not to open it unless he doesn't return.

....

B The present (2)

questions and negatives

1 Read the following explanations of how to make questions and negatives with present tense verbs.

present tense questions and negatives

1 We make questions by changing the order of the *subject* and the *auxiliary verb*:
STATEMENT: *Anya **is studying** English.*
QUESTIONS: ***Is** Anya **studying** English?*
*Why **is** Anya **studying** English?*
*What **is** Anya **studying**?*

2 If the verb does not have an auxiliary (in the statement) we use ***do*** before the subject to make questions:
STATEMENT: *Kevin **lives** in Sydney.*
QUESTIONS: ***Does** Kevin **live** in Sydney?*
*Why **does Kevin** live in Sydney?*
*Where **does Kevin** live?*

3 When we answer a question we often use the *short form* with the auxiliary ***do/does*** or ***don't/doesn't***:
*'**Do** the girls **like** the new house?' 'Yes, they **do**.'*
*'**Does** John **live** in Oxford?' 'No, he **doesn't**.'*
If the question uses the auxiliary ***be***, we repeat the auxiliary in the answer:
*'**Is** Jenny a trainee?' 'No, she **isn't**.'*
*'**Are** we very busy today?' 'Yes, we **are**.'*

4 We make negative sentences by putting ***not*** after the auxiliary verb or after ***do***:
STATEMENT: *Anya **is studying** English.*
*Kevin **lives** in Sydney.*
NEGATIVE: *Anya **is not** (**isn't**) studying English.*
*Kevin **does not** (**doesn't**) live in Sydney.*

2 Rearrange the words to make questions about Marek, the sculptor (see Exercise 2 in Section A). The first one is done for you. Don't forget the question mark.

a does/live/Marek/where
Where does Marek live?

b does/every morning/get up/he/when
....

c does/get/he/how/to work
....

d at the moment/he/is/working on/what
....

e for this sculpture/he/is/using/why/wood
....

f at work/does/he/wear/what
....

g does/have/he/supper/where
....

h are/book/they/reading/what
....

i does/he/watch television/who/with
....

j about/at this moment/dreaming/he/is/what
....

3 **Look back at Exercise 2 in Section A. Are the following statements *True* (T) or *False* (F)? If they are *False*, correct them. The first one is done for you.**

a He gets up at eight o'clock every morning.
F – He doesn't. He gets up at about six o'clock.

b Marek lives in London.

c He goes to work by bus.

d He wears a suit and tie to work.

e He is making a wooden sculpture.

f He is working in his studio today.

g He has dinner by himself.

h He is reading *Mary Poppins* to his children.

i He and his wife listen to the radio every evening.

j He dreams of all the sculptures he is going to make one day.

4 **Make questions and replies about the following information, using the present simple or present continuous. In the replies use a pronoun to replace the name or noun in the question. (✓ = reply with Yes; ✗ = reply with No.)**

a Paul/like/jogging. ✓
Does Paul like jogging?
Yes, he does.

b swimming/be/good for you ✓

c the girls' team/training/this afternoon ✗

d the tennis tournament/be/in July ✓

e the sports coaches/work/in the summer ✗

f sportsmen and sportswomen/need/lots of sleep ✓

g rowing a boat/be/good exercise ✓

h people/need/lots of protein ✗

i Paul/change/his shoes/at the moment ✓

j Jenny/need/new trainers ✓

k the gym/be/open on Sundays ✗

l Jenny/run/round the track now ✗

m Olive/want/a sauna after the race ✓

n the team/compete/in this tournament ✗

C Mixed practice

present simple • present continuous

1 Choose the correct form of the verb in brackets and fill the gaps.

Kim is in her final year of a psychology degree at the University of East Anglia in England. Her final exams (**a** be) .... next week so there are no classes. Like all the other students on her course this week she (**b** revise) .... But Kim (**c** not study) .... very hard right now. She (**d** sit) .... in the garden of her house (**e** read) .... her notes. It is a beautiful day. Birds (**f** sing) .... in the trees. She (**g** sit/not/usually) .... in the garden like this during term time. Normally she (**h** take) .... the bus to the university at nine o'clock and (**i** study) .... all day. She (**j** have) .... lunch at about one with her friends, usually Alice and Gemma. But today Alice (**k** visit) .... her grandmother and Gemma (**l** take) .... part in an athletics event. Still Kim's brother is home from his job as a junior doctor in Scotland. She can hear him now. He (**m** talk) .... to his girlfriend on the telephone. The sun (**n** get) .... hotter. Maybe revising is not such a good idea. Perhaps she could ring Alice and they could go for a swim.

2 Write the most appropriate form of the verbs (in brackets) in the gaps. Jacky Beadle is talking on the telephone about the man she works for.

a Yes, Malcolm Clarke .....is..... a member of staff here. (be)

b I'm sorry Mr Clarke isn't here. He .... a conference in Warsaw. (attend)

c He usually .... in his office from nine till three. (work)

d Yes, Mr Clarke .... to quite a lot of conferences. (go)

e At the conference in Warsaw, they .... global warming. (discuss)

f Yes, Mr Clarke .... global warming is a problem. Why? Because it .... warmer all the time. (believe; get)

g He .... here for about six months of the year, and the rest of the time he .... around the world. (live; travel)

h He usually .... by plane. (go)

i He .... at the Meridien hotel in Warsaw. (stay)

j I don't know, but I hope that he .... a good time. (have)

k No, I'm sorry. I .... questions like that. We .... people's phone numbers or addresses. (not/answer; not/give)

3 **Use the following prompts to make some of the caller's questions (from the previous exercise) about Mr Clarke. The first one is done for you.**

a Malcolm Clarke – a member of staff there?

Is Malcolm Clarke a member of staff there?

b at work – when?

....

c discussing in Warsaw – what?

....

d Mr Clarke – believe – global warming is a problem?

....

e he – global warming is a problem – why?

....

f Mr Clarke – travel a lot?

....

g he travel – how?

....

h staying in Warsaw – where?

....

i Mr Clarke – have a good time?

....

4 **Jacky is having coffee with her sister Sarah. She is talking about her boss (Mr Clarke). Write the verbs from the box in the correct gaps, using the appropriate present tense (the first one is done for you).**

not be	live
not drive	make
not enjoy	realise
feel	seem
get	speak
go	take
grow	take part
have	travel
leave (x2)	visit
like (x3)	

'He (**a**) ......*lives*...... in North London with his wife (a doctor), two children, a dog and a cat. He (**b**)................. a taxi to work every day because he (**c**) ....; he (**d**) .... it, you see.

He (**e**) .... a lot. He (**f**) .... all our overseas offices. At the moment he (**g**) .... in a conference in Warsaw. He (**h**) .... about pollution and the environment.

Everybody really (**i**) .... Malcolm, but he is a bit forgetful. He (**j**) .... his things on trains or in taxis. When he (**k**) .... that he's left some papers or his briefcase in some car or on some train he (**l**) .... crazy and we (**m**) .... to start telephoning all over London – well all over the world, sometimes – to try and find his things. But he (**n**) .... stupid. He just (**o**) .... to be. Actually he's pretty clever.

The reason why everybody (**p**) .... Malcolm? Well, you see, the company (**q**) .... all the time. We're (**r**) .... big plans for the future, and everybody (**s**) .... very optimistic. We know that's because of Malcolm. He often (**t**) .... brilliant ideas and everybody (**u**) .... him a lot – I've said that already, haven't I!

That's why we're all a bit sad. He (**v**) .... the company in two weeks. He's going to travel the world and write a novel. Sounds OK to me.

UNIT 2

A The past (1)

past simple • past continuous

1 Read the following descriptions of the form and use of the past simple.

past simple – form

1 The past simple of regular verbs is formed by adding *-ed* to the *base form* of the verb:
walk → ***walked*** *jump* → ***jumped***
though many common verbs have irregular past simple forms:
buy → ***bought*** *see* → ***saw***

2 We form questions in the past simple by adding the *auxiliary* ***did*** before the subject of the verb:
Did *the doctor* ***get*** *to the meeting in time?*
Did *Annette* ***win*** *the prize?*

3 We form the negative of the past simple by adding ***did*** + ***not*** or ***n't*** before the base form of the verb:
The animals ***did not stay*** *in the field.*
David ***didn't finish*** *his sentence.*

past simple – use

4 We use the past simple to talk about single, complete events in the past:
She ***came*** *round the corner of the house and saw the lorry.*
France ***won*** *the World Cup.*

5 We use the past simple to talk about repeated events in the past:
She ***wrote*** *to him once a week.*
She ***went*** *to work by car every day.*

6 We use the past simple to talk about a situation that continued for some time in the past but is now finished:
We ***lived*** *in the country at that time.*
She ***studied*** *philosophy for three years*

Now look at this description of the form and use of the past continuous.

past continuous – form

7 The past continuous is formed with the past form of the verb ***be*** and the ***-ing*** form of the main verb:
Jean ***was playing*** *the clarinet.*
The nurses ***were singing*** *in the children's ward.*

8 We form questions by putting the *auxiliary* before the *subject*:
Was *Jean* ***playing*** *the flute?*
What ***were*** *the nurses* ***singing?***

9 The negative is formed by adding ***not*** or ***n't*** to the auxiliary:
She ***wasn't playing*** *the guitar.*
Weren't *they* ***singing*** *very loud?*

past continuous – use

10 We use the past continuous to talk about actions which were in progress at a particular time in the past:
I ***was playing*** *in the garden at ten o'clock.*
She ***was studying*** *for her exams yesterday evening.*

Remember: there are certain verbs that are not usually used in the continuous, such as verbs describing feelings (e.g. ***want***, ***like***, ***hate***, ***hope***) and other *stative* verbs such as ***remember***, ***recognise***, ***belong*** (see Unit 1, Section A, Exercise 1, point 4).

2 Write either the past simple or past continuous form of the verbs in brackets. The first one is done for you.

It (**a** be) ......was...... 6.15. In the Adelphi Theatre the actors (**b** arrive) .... for the evening performance. It (**c** raining) .... outside. Jack Long, the caretaker, (**d** sweep) .... the corridor when he (**e** hear) .... a loud voice. He (**f** look) .... around. On the stage a young woman (**g** stand) .... in the darkness, (**h** speak) .... loudly. When she (**i** notice) .... the caretaker, she (**j** stop) .... and (**k** run) .... off the stage. 'What (**l** you/do) .... ?' he (**m** shout) ....
The girl (**n** say) .... , 'I'm sorry. I (**o** pass) .... the theatre and the door (**p** is) .... open. I've never been on a stage before and I really (**q** want) .... to try it. I just want to be an actress!

3 There are some mistakes in the past tense verbs in these sentences. Underline them and write the correct form. If there is no mistake write *correct*. The first one is done for you.

a This morning I <u>was arriving</u> at work at exactly ten past nine. ......arrived......

b The train was being late. ....

c When I got to the office the manager opened his door and was calling me. ....

d I was going into his office immediately. ....

e I apologised for being late ... .

f ... and just as I went out of the door ....

g ... he said 'by the way, the management decided yesterday to promote you to district manager.' ....

h I was being really amazed! ....

4 Look at the pictures. Which picture do the sentences below belong to? The first one is done for you.

1

2

3

4

a A man and a woman were walking, exhausted, in a desert. ......picture 1......

b He looked down and saw two people. ....

c But when they got there it disappeared. ....

d They were collapsing and were clearly near to death. ....

e It was a mirage. ....

f Later that same day, towards evening, a pilot was flying his light aircraft low over the desert. ....

g They saw an oasis and hurried towards it. ....

h He managed to land and help the exhausted couple into his plane. ....

i They didn't have any water left. ....

B The past (2)

past perfect

1 **Read the following explanation of the past perfect.**

past perfect – form

1 The past perfect is made by using the *auxiliary* ***had*** or ***'d*** and the *past participle*:
Janet ***had climbed*** *that hill before.*
The teachers ***had*** *already* ***left*** *the hall.*
He was sure that ***he'd paid*** *the bill.*

2 The negative is formed by adding ***no*** or ***n't*** to the auxiliary verb:
Sara ***hadn't met*** *Colin before.*
Liam and Stephanie ***hadn't finished*** *their dinner when Joe arrived.*

3 We form questions by changing the position of the *subject* of the verb and the auxiliary:
Had *the train* ***gone****?*
Where ***had*** *Monica* ***left*** *her keys?*

past perfect – use

4 The past perfect is used to talk about something that took place before another past event or situation:
Sam walked into his sitting room and saw that someone ***had painted*** *it green.*
When I arrived at the station, the train ***had gone****.*

Note: if we want to use more than one verb with the same subject in the past perfect we only need to use the auxiliary once:
Ned ***had picked up*** *the box,* ***opened*** *it, and* ***thrown*** *the contents away.*

2 **Read the following story. Underline the past tense verbs in each sentence and circle the event that happened first. The first one is done for you.**

a When David got home he saw that someone had left the front door open.
b He wondered what on earth had happened.
c He noticed that someone had made a lot of footprints in the flowerbed.
d He was sure that he'd locked the door that morning.
e He was horrified to see that someone had smashed the window.
f David guessed that a burglar had broken in.
g He went into the sitting room and saw that the clock on the wall had gone.
h The burglar had not had time to take everything because David came home.
i When he had looked around the house he phoned the police.
j He told them exactly what the burglar had taken.
k The police said that he had done the right thing.
l He hadn't touched anything before he called them.
m They hoped that the damage had not been too serious.
n After he had finished the phone call he made himself a cup of tea.
o He was glad they hadn't taken the kettle!

3 **Put the verbs in brackets into the past perfect or past simple to make the order of events clear. The first one is done for you.**

a When he (make) his decision he (go) to talk to the manager.
When he had made his decision he went to talk to the manager.

b He (work) at the company for ten years when he (retire).
....

c He (can not) get into his flat because he (forget) his keys.
....

d I (not eat) since the morning so I (be) really hungry by eight o'clock.
....

e When she (wash and change) she (call) a taxi.
....

f She (want) to visit Rome because she (read) a lot about it.
....

g They (arrive) late because they (miss) the bus.
....

4 **Answer the following questions according to the Yes/No cue. Use contracted forms where you can. The first one is done for you.**

a 'Was Grace sure she had posted a letter to Barry three days ago?'
'No, *she wasn't sure she'd posted a letter to him.*'

b 'Had Barry got a letter from Grace?'
'No, ...'

c 'Did Grace hope that she had not posted a letter to Barry?'
'Yes, ...'

d 'Had Barry remembered to check the post recently?'
'No, ...'

e 'Had Grace accepted a new job in a foreign country?'
'Yes, ...'

f 'Had Barry heard about Grace's new job?'
'No, ...'

g 'Was Grace sure that she had made the right decision?'
'No, ...'

h 'Had Barry asked Grace to marry him three days ago?'
'Yes, ...'

i 'Had Grace agreed to marry him?'
'Yes, ...'

What was in Grace's letter do you think?

C Mixed practice

past simple • past continuous • past perfect

1 Complete the verb table. The first one is done for you.

infinitive	past form	past participle
a arrive	*arrived*	*arrived*
b be		
c bring		
d buy		
e do		
f eat		
g feel		
h get		
i have		

infinitive	past form	past participle
j see		
k meet		
l know		
m ring		
n send		
o start		
p drink		
q tell		

2 Make questions using the prompts in brackets and the question word in blue. The first one is done for you.

a (Tim asked you something then)
what *What did Tim ask you then?*

b (he had come over to speak to you)
why ....

c (he was talking about something)
what ....

d (Diana got there)
when ....

e (you first saw Tim)
when ....

f (you said something)
what ....

g (you said that)
why ....

h (you thought something about that)
what ....

i (you were waiting for someone)
who ....

3 **Now here are the answers to the questions in the Exercise 2. Choose the question that goes with each answer and write it in the correct space. The first one is done for you.**

a ....Question e........
– My second week in college. I was waiting for someone in the canteen when he came in.

b ....
– Diana, a friend of mine.

c ....
– About ten minutes later. But Tim was talking to me when she came in.

d ....
– I can't remember.

e ....
– Because he thought I looked 'interesting'.

f ....
– Not much!

g ....
– He asked me to go to the cinema with him.

h ....
– I told him no.

i ....
– Because I'd already seen the film

4 **Read the following story and complete the tasks below.**

Alison decided to go hill walking. She didn't tell anyone where she planned to go. When she reached the top of the first hill she looked for her map. She thought she had packed it in her jacket pocket, but it wasn't there. Suddenly a thick fog came down over the hills, and she couldn't see anything. She tried to find her way home, but she kept coming back to the same place. She was beginning to get very frightened. As she was stumbling along in the fog her foot went down a hole. It hurt terribly and she fainted. She had broken her ankle.

Back at home Alison's flatmate, Serena, was getting worried. It was dark and Alison still hadn't come home. Serena was afraid something had happened to her friend. At ten o'clock Serena rang the mountain rescue service.

When Alison woke up it was light and she was freezing cold. She realised she had been there all night. She heard a helicopter and she waved and shouted for help, but it was useless.

The search party didn't know where Alison had been. They had searched the whole area and they were exhausted. Just when they had decided to give up and go home, one of them saw a hand waving. It was Alison. She had crawled out of her hole and she was shouting for help. And the moral of the story? Don't forget your map when you go out alone and always tell someone where you are going.

a Underline all the past tense verbs in the story.

b How many past simple verbs are there? ....

c How many past continuous verbs are there? ....

d How many past perfect verbs are there? ....

e Cover the text of the story. Write Alison's story in your own words without looking back at the text.

UNIT 3

A Quantifiers (1)

quantifiers with countable nouns

1 Read the explanations of how we use quantifiers (*no*, *few* etc.) with countable nouns. Remember, countable nouns are those which can be singular and plural, such as *book – books*, *person – people*, *home – homes*.

quantifier + countable

1 ***No*** is usually used in positive statements with *plural* nouns:

*There were **no policemen** outside the stadium.*

No is used with *singular* nouns in formal English:

***No person** may enter the room during an exam.*

*He promised that **no reasonable offer** would be refused.*

2 ***A few*** is used with plural nouns and has a positive meaning (like ***some***):

*Harry always kept **a few sweets** in his pocket.*

Few is used with plural nouns but has a negative meaning (like ***not many***). It is often used with ***very***. (Note: ***few*** is quite formal and not very common in spoken English; usually, we use ***not many***.)

***Few people** enjoy exams.*

3 ***Some*** is used with plural nouns in positive and negative statements:

***Some cities** are cleaner than others.*

Some is also used in offers and requests:

*Would you like to borrow **some CDs**?*

*Could I have **some potatoes** please?*

4 ***Any*** is used with plural nouns in questions and in negative statements:

*Have you had **any emails** today?*

*I don't want **any biscuits**, thank you.*

Any can also be used when stressed in positive statements:

*I will accept **any offers** of help.*

5 ***Many*** is used with plural nouns, usually in negative statements and in questions:

***Not many people** came to see the show.*

*Are there **many students** in the class?*

We sometimes use ***many*** in positive statements in formal language:

***Many department stores** give large discounts.*

In positive statements we usually use ***a lot of*** (often with ***quite***) instead of ***many***. (**Note:** ***a lot of*** is more formal than ***lots of***, which is used in casual speech.)

*There were (quite) **a lot of boats** on the lake.*

6 ***Most*** is used with plural nouns to mean '**almost all**':

***Most shops** have increased their prices this season.*

7 ***All*** is used with plural nouns:

***All apples** are delicious.*

8 ***Every*** is used with singular nouns:

*Tom goes to the gym **every day**.*

quantifier + *of*

9 All these quantifiers, apart from ***no*** and ***every***, are often used with ***of*** + *determiner* (***the***, ***this***, ***that***, ***my***, ***our***, ***them*** etc.) when we want to talk about something specific:

*Della bought **some of the** most expensive boots in the shop.*

All can be used with or without ***of***:

*She gave her sister **all of her** CDs./She gave her sister **all her** CDs.*

All cannot be used without ***of*** before a pronoun:

*She gave her sister **all of them**.*

Note: ***no*** changes to ***none*** when followed by ***of*** + *determiner*:

***None of the** shoes were in her size.*

2 **Look at the following sentences about shopping in Britain. Add a quantifier from the explanations above according to the quantity indicated on the right. The first one is done for you.**

a ..Most.... people shop in supermarkets.

b .... goods are sold cheaply to make sure people buy them.

c .... families go shopping on Sundays.

d .... people buy things in small village shops nowadays.

e Not .... shoplifters get sent to prison.

f .... supermarket companies try to improve the areas they build in.

g .... supermarkets offer very little choice.

h Some prices are reduced .... Saturday afternoon.

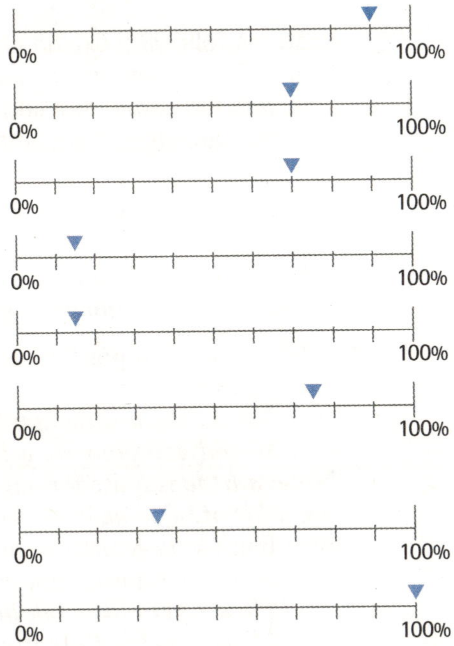

3 **Look at the picture and choose the right words from the box to complete the sentences describing the scene.**

any	most
lot of	a few
many	no
all	some
a lot of	lots of

a There are .... coats on the rack.

b There aren't .... trousers.

c .... shirts are hanging on the rack.

d Next to the coats there are .... dresses.

e On the table there are .... socks for sale.

f There are quite a .... handkerchiefs.

g There aren't .... gloves left.

h There are still .... hats.

i .... the hats are black.

j .... of the scarves are red.

k There are .... blue gloves.

B Quanitifiers (2)

quantifiers with uncountable nouns

1 Read the following explanations of how these quantifiers are used with uncountable nouns. Remember, uncountable nouns are those which do not normally have a plural form with the same meaning, such as *milk*, *information*, *cotton* etc. Notice that we do not use *a few*, *few*, *many* and *every* with uncountable nouns.

quantifier + uncountable

1 *No* is used with uncountable nouns in positive statements:
*Ken had absolutely **no chance** of winning.*
*Ken had **no money** in his wallet.*

2 *A little* is used in positive statements, offers and requests:
*Ursula has **a little jam** left on her plate.*
*Would you pour me **a little milk**?*
Note: ***a little*** is quite formal and we usually use ***a bit of*** or ***some*** in spoken English.
We often use ***very little*** to mean '**almost none**', and ***too little*** to mean '**not enough**':
*There's **very little ink** in the printer.*
*There was **too little time** to finish the test.*

3 *Some* is usually used in positive statements:
***Some jam** has colouring added.*
Some is also often used in offers and requests:
*Would you like **some milk** in your tea?*
*Can I have **some information**, please?*
Note: ***a bit of*** is used in informal speech to mean '**some**':
*I really like **a bit of jam** on my toast.*
*Jack, our dog, caused **a bit of trouble** in the shop.*

4 *Any* is used in questions and negatives:
*Have you got **any change** in your pocket?*
I've only got a £10 note.
*There isn't **any** cough **medicine**.*
Any can also be used when stressed in positive statements:
*I'll take **any advice** you can give me.*

5 *A lot of* is usually used in positive statements and questions:
***A lot of butter** is imported from abroad.*
*I hate carrying **a lot of luggage**.*
*Is there **a lot of salt** in the soup?*
Note: ***A lot of*** is more formal than ***lots of***, which is used in casual speech:
*Keith likes **lots of sugar** in his tea.*

6 *Much* is usually used in questions and in negatives:
*Is there **much tea** left?*
*How **much bread** do we need for the sandwiches?*
*We don't need **much butter**.*
In positive statements, ***much*** is more formal than ***a lot of*** and is not often used:
*There was **much shouting** and **laughter** when the clowns entered.*
However, we use ***much*** with ***so*** quite often in positive statements:
*Tom bought **so much paper** he had nowhere to put it.*
*I never knew there was **so much juice** in a lemon.*

7 *Most* is used in positive statements and questions:
***Most office furniture** is made of metal.*
*Where is **most sugar** produced?*

8 *All* is used in positive statements and questions:
***All pasta** is made from wheat.*
*Does **all tea** come from China?*

quantifier + of + the, this, that

9 All these *quantifiers*, apart from **no**, are often used with ***of*** + *determiner* (***the***, ***this***, ***that***, ***his***, ***our***, ***them*** etc.) when we want to talk about a part of something specific:
***Some of his** coffee spilt on the floor.*
*Have you eaten **any of that** marmalade I bought?*
***Most of the** land around the river was flooded.*
*Can I offer you **a little of this** French cheese?*
*I haven't read **much of the** paper.*
All can be used with or without *of*:
*Janet drank **all** (**of**) **the orange juice**.*
*The sun melted **all** (**of**) **the snow**.*
However, you must use *of* before a pronoun:
*She finished **all of it**.*

2 Look at the following 'quantity line' and then choose the appropriate quantifier for each group of sentences (a–f).

No/(not)any	not much/a little	a bit of/some	a lot of/much	most	all
0%					100%

a How .... milk is there in the fridge?
There isn't .... hope for you!
Pauline didn't have .... time for relaxation.

b .... fruit is good for you!
Gregory thought that .... maths was dull.
Polly finished .... the trifle and .... the lemonade.

c I'm afraid there's .... flour left for pancakes.
There's .... water in the swimming pool during winter.
John was so busy he had .... time to chat on the phone.

d I enjoyed .... of the music in the show.
.... people need reading glasses when they become middle-aged.
Robin and Sue like .... Japanese food, but not raw fish.

e Look! There's .... gravy on the carpet!
We often have .... fish on a Friday evening.
You need .... sugar in the mixture. It's a bit too sour.

f There's .... fat in fried food.
.... the coffee we drink is imported from South America.
You'll need .... paint to cover that huge wall!

3 Two friends are preparing a meal. Choose a quantifier from the box to complete their conversation.

a bit (x2)	lots
a little	lots of
all	much (x2)
any (x2)	no
few	some

ROBERT: Don't put too (**a**) .... oil in the pan. You only need (**b**) .... bit.
PATRICK: Oh, I think you need (**c**) .... of oil.
ROBERT: Well OK, but just not too (**d**) .... , OK?
PATRICK: Don't worry. I'm not going to go crazy.
ROBERT: I'm glad to hear it! Now you have to add (**e**) .... onions.
PATRICK: But I don't want to put (**f**) .... onions in this. I don't like them.
ROBERT: Oh no, you don't, do you. I suppose that's OK.
PATRICK: Do I need to use (**g**) .... the tomatoes?
ROBERT: No, you only need a (**h**) ....
PATRICK: Shall I put in (**i**) .... of oregano?
ROBERT: Yes. That would be great. I like to use (**j**) .... herbs.
PATRICK: OK. And what's next?
ROBERT: Salt! We need (**k**) .... of salt – not much.
PATRICK: Where is it?
ROBERT: Where's what?
PATRICK: The salt. There's (**l**) .... salt anywhere.
ROBERT: Didn't you buy (**m**) .... ?
PATRICK: No. I thought you were going to.
ROBERT: Oh no!

C Mixed practice quantifiers with countable and uncountable nouns

1 Rewrite the statements using quantifiers to reflect your point of view. The first one is done for you.

a Boys like football.

A lot of boys like football, but not all of them do. A few aren't interested at all.

b Girls are interested in fashion.

....

....

c Young people like discos.

....

....

d Young people don't like school.

....

....

e People think films are more interesting than plays at the theatre.

....

....

f Old people watch television every evening.

....

....

2 Draw a smiley face (☺) or a sad face (☹) for each sentence. The first one is done for you.

a A few people really like my new paintings. ☺

b Every time I talk to her she smiles. ○

c Few people came to my party. ○

d I have very little chance of passing this exam. ○

e I'm not having much fun right now. ○

f A lot of people really like my pictures. ○

g My friend Elaine had little opportunity to visit me. ○

h There are a lot of people in here. They've all come to see my paintings. ○

i There are so many questions in the exam. I'm certain to get some of them right. ○

j Very few people like my new paintings. ○

3 Correct the mistakes in the following sentences. The first one is done for you.

a We don't get much shoppers here any more.
We don't get many shoppers here any more.

b People spend very few money in this shop.

c This will only take little time.

d There aren't any sugar in this tin.

e Every people likes coffee.

f I always drink coffee after all meal.

g I only take a few milk in my coffee.

h I'll come round in a little minutes.

i Finding a good bargain in the shops gives me many satisfaction.

4 Look at the results of a survey about what people have for breakfast in a city in Ireland. Complete the sentences using the information in the survey.

What people drink:	What people eat:
44% tea	55% cereal (cornflakes, muesli)
41% coffee	23% toast
7% fruit juice	11% cooked breakfasts (fried bacon, egg, sausage)
3% milk	7% no breakfast
3% water	4% boiled eggs
2% nothing	

a A few people eat ……………

b A few people drink ……………

c A lot of people eat ……………

d Most people eat ……………

e Some people drink ……………

f Not many people eat ……………

g Most people drink ……………

A Comparatives and superlatives (1)

regular forms of comparatives and superlatives

1 **Read the explanations.**

1 To form the *comparative* of a *short adjective* or *adverb* we add ***-er*** + ***than***:
*Keith is **taller than** Bob.*
*Bob's house is **grander than** mine.*
*Mike ran **faster than** Tom.*
To form the *superlative* we add ***(the) -est*** to the adjective or adverb:
*Sally is **the tallest** girl in the class.*
*This pair of shoes is **the cheapest** in the shop.*

2 If the short adjective or adverb ends in a *single vowel* and a *consonant* (except *w*) we double the consonant and add ***-er*** or ***-est***:
*hot → **hotter** → (the) **hottest***
*mad → **madder** → (the) **maddest***

3 If an adjective or an adverb ends in a consonant and an *e* we add ***-r*** or ***–st***:
*large → **larger** → (the) **largest***
*fine → **finer** → (the) **finest***

4 If the adjective or adverb has two *syllables* and ends in a consonant sound we usually use ***more***, ***(the) most***:
*serious → **more** serious → **(the) most** serious*
*patient → **more** patient → **(the) most** patient*
But if it ends in a *vowel* sound or ***l*** or ***r*** sound we usually add *-(e)r*, *–(e)st*:
*yellow → **yellower** → (the) **yellowest***
*little → **littler** → (the) **littlest***

5 If the adjective ends in *-y* we change it to *-i* and add ***-er*** or ***-est***:
*pretty → **prettier** → (the) **prettiest***
*ugly → **uglier** → (the) **ugliest***
But if an adverb ends in ***-ly*** we add ***more*** or ***(the) most*** before it:
*sadly → **more** sadly → **(the) most** sadly*
*quickly → **more** quickly → **(the) most** quickly*

6 If the adjective or adverb has more than two syllables we add ***more*** for the comparative, and ***(the) most*** for the superlative:
*exciting → **more** exciting → **(the) most** exciting*
*monotonous → **more** monotonous → **(the) most** monotonous*

7 If we want to say that the difference between two things is very great we use ***much*** or ***far*** + comparative + ***than***:
*Lennie runs **much faster than** I do.*
*She is **far fitter than** me.*

2 Read the following dialogue and indicate which of the above rules the adjective or adverb is following in each sentence. The first one is done for you.

a That was *the most delicious* meal I have ever eaten!
rule 6

b It is *the newest* restaurant in the area. ....

c The service is good. They brought the meal *more quickly* here.
....

d That dessert we had at Mario's last week was *richer*.
....

e Yes, I thought the dessert was *lighter* here. ....

f But I think Luigi's looks *nicer* ... .

g ... and it must be *the busiest* restaurant in town. ....

h I think the menu is *bigger* here, though. ....

i The *most important* question is – which is *the most expensive*!
....

3 Look at the pictures of the three hotels and write two sentences comparing them, using one comparative and one superlative and the word in the brackets. The first one is done for you.

a (expensive) The Regent is more expensive than the Hotel Mario. The Majestic is probably the most expensive.

b (comfortable) ....

c (noisy) ....

d (modern) ....

e (crowded) ....

f (cheap) ....

g (luxurious) ....

h (peaceful) ....

i (attractive) ....

B Comparatives and superlatives (2)

irregular forms, and other ways of comparing

1 **Read the following explanations of irregular comparatives and superlatives and other ways of making comparisons.**

irregular comparative and superlative adjectives and adverbs

1 Many of the most common *adjectives* and *adverbs* have *irregular comparative* and *superlative* forms:
good → ***better*** → *(the)* ***best***
well → ***better*** → *(the)* ***best***
bad → ***worse*** → *(the)* ***worst***
badly → ***worse*** → *(the)* ***worst***
far → ***further/farther*** → *(the)* ***farthest****/(the)* ***furthest***
old → ***older/elder*** → *(the)* ***oldest/eldest***
Note: we only use ***elder*** and ***the eldest*** to refer to people, and not to things.

2 The *quantifiers* ***little***, ***much***, ***many*** and ***few*** have irregular comparatives:
little → ***less*** → *(the)* ***least***
much/many → ***more*** → *(the)* ***most***
few → ***fewer*** or ***less*** → ***fewest*** or *(the)* ***least***

common comparative expressions

3 When we want to indicate something is getting progressively more or less, we repeat the comparative with ***and***:
The water was getting ***deeper and deeper****.*
It was raining ***more and more heavily****.*

4 To compare things in a negative way we use ***less*** *…* ***than***:
Tom was ***less*** *optimistic* ***than*** *Andy.* (= Andy was more optimistic.)
We also use ***not as*** *…* ***as*** for a negative comparison:
Bill ***isn't as*** *successful* ***as*** *his brother.* (= His brother is more successful.)
He ***doesn't*** *work* ***as*** *hard* ***as*** *him.*

5 To compare two equal, or nearly equal, things we use ***as*** *…* ***as***:
Antonia is ***as*** *tall* ***as*** *Jane.*
Jane is almost ***as*** *confident* ***as*** *Karen.*

6 We can qualify comparatives with adverbials such as ***a bit***, ***a lot***, ***much*** and ***far*** before the comparative form:
Ken was ***a bit fatter than*** *before.*
The Strong family are ***far richer than*** *their neighbours.*
We can qualify superlatives with ***by far***:
The footballer was ***by far the richest*** *man at the party.*
For negative comparisons we can also use ***not nearly*** *…* ***as*** *…* ***as***, and ***far less*** *…* ***than***:
Helen ***isn't nearly as generous as*** *Elizabeth.*
Bernard was ***far less amusing than*** *David.*

7 We can make phrases using comparatives with …… ***the better***:
The sooner ***the better****.*
The bigger ***the better****.*

8 To indicate that two things change at the same rate we use ***the*** *…****er*** ***the*** *…****er***, or ***the more*** *…* ***the more*** *…*:
The older *I get* ***the better*** *I understand.*
The more *patient William is* ***the more*** *angry Mary gets.*
We can mix the negative and the positive comparison:
The faster *the car is,* ***the less*** *fuel-efficient it is.*
The more *fragrant the rose is,* ***the less*** *beautiful.*

2 **Add a phrase so that the new sentences mean the same as the old ones. The first one is done for you.**

a Really hot coffee is the best. — The hotter the better.

b Linda has three younger sisters. — Linda is ……………

c The hotel is less crowded this year than it was last month and the month before. — It's getting ……………

d The station is more dirty every week. — The station is getting …………… ……………

e The family is very happy in their new house. They used to be very unhappy. — They're much …………… ……………

f Really cheap markets are the best. — …………… the better.

g The doctor earns a lot more than the nurse. — The nurse doesn't …………… ……………

h The sofa is very expensive and so are the two chairs. — It's ……………

i Traffic is much safer when it goes slowly. — The …………… it goes, …………… it is.

3 **Look at the picture and put the missing words in the following sentences.**

a Aunt Jane is …………… taller …………… Aunt Lucinda.

b Cousin Jack's hair is nearly …………… long …………… Phillip's.

c Delia has …………… bigger teeth ……………Frances.

d Grandma is …………… older …………… Phillip.

e The twins are …………… fat …………… each other.

f Mark is …………… thinner …………… Phillip.

g Grandpa is …………… as bald …………… Uncle George.

h Aunt Jane is …………… the oldest woman in the family.

i Uncle George is the …………… dressed man in the family.

j Delia is the …………… dressed woman in the family.

k Mark is much …………… frightening …………… Jack.

l Frances is …………… person in the family.

C Mixed practice comparative and superlative adverbs and adjectives

1 Complete the adjective and adverb tables. The first two are done for you.

Adjective	Comparative form	Superlative form
a cold	*colder*	*the coldest*
b angry		
c honest		
d pale		
e good		
f emotional		
g kind		
h sad		
i blue		

Adverb	Comparative form	Superlative form
j fast		
k slowly		
l well		
m kindly		
n badly		
o often		
p much		
q early		
r frequently		

2 Look at the pictures and write a sentence comparing the things or people in the pictures.

a The white shoes are ....

b The short girl can run ....

c John is ....

d The girl in the T-shirt must be ....

e The house on the left is ....

f The road on the right looks ....

3 **Complete the following exchanges with the phrases in the box. The first one is done for you.**

a bit more difficult
and more exciting
as he is
hotter and hotter
as much as
much more interesting
the better
the bigger
the easiest
less than

a 'Why are you going inside?'
'It's getting *hotter and hotter*! I can't stand it.'

b 'You seem to be enjoying that book.'
'Yes. It's .... than I had expected.'

c 'When are you going to finish putting up those shelves?'
'As soon as I can. It's .... than I expected.'

d 'You can't hear yourself speak in here.'
'Great! The noisier ....'

e 'You don't want coffee? I thought you liked coffee.'
'Not .... I used to.'

f 'Why don't you want to play cards with your brother?'
'I'm not as good at cards ....'

g 'The meals here are absolutely enormous.'
'Great! .... the better!'

h 'Isn't it all too expensive?'
'Oh no. You can get a flight for .... £65.'

i 'How did you get on in the exam?'
'Great. It was .... one of all of them.'

j 'Why are you so keen on that television programme?'
'Because it's getting more ....'

4 **Add one phrase from each of the two columns to make a sentence. You can only use each phrase once.**

as keen on holidays as	a bit wiser.
it's hotter in December	better.
more and more crowded	cities in the world.
more fun than	cruises.
more expensive	every year.
one of the most famous	her sister.
tall as	his sister.
the	I've ever had.
was the best one	than going by train.
we get	than in July.

a Brian isn't as ....

b Camping holidays are ....

c Flying is ....

d Heat? The hotter ....

e In Australia ....

f Last year's holiday ....

g Paris is ....

h She's not ....

i The roads are getting ....

j Every year ....

UNIT 5

A Present perfect

form and use; *never, often, ever*, etc.

1 Read the following explanations.

present perfect – form

1 The present perfect simple is formed by using the *auxiliary* ***has/have*** with the *past participle* of the main verb:

*I **have found** your gloves.*
*He **has left** for the airport.*

In conversation we often contract the auxiliary to ***'s/'ve***, particularly after pronouns (e.g. ***I, he, they***):

I've found ... He's left ...

We make the negative by adding ***not*** or ***n't*** after the auxiliary **have:**

*Robin **has not seen** the film 'Lord of the Rings'!*
*John **hasn't mended** the computer yet.*

Note: When we are answering a question in the present perfect we can use the short *yes/no* answer with the auxiliary ***have***:

*'**Have** you **found** your scarf?' – 'Yes, I **have**.'*

Exception: the verb **go** changes to ***has been*** in the present perfect when we mean **'visited'**:

*My mother **has been** to America.*
(= She has visited America.)

but: *My mother **has gone** to America.*
(= She is in America now.)

present perfect – use

2 We use the present perfect when we talk about something that started in the past and is still the case:

*Phil **has known** his friend Ross since they were seven.*

3 We use the present perfect to talk about something that happened in the past but that has consequences in the present:

*He **has bought** a new computer (so he is selling his old one).*

4 We use the present perfect when we talk about things that happened in a period of time that is not yet finished (e.g. ***today, this week***):

*He **has had** three driving lessons this month.*

never, often, just, already, ever

5 With the present perfect we often use ***never, often, just*** and ***already***:

*Helen **has never been** to France.*
*She **has often forgotten** her door key.*
*David **has just found** some money on the pavement.*
*Has Paul **already arrived**?*

We use ***ever*** in questions and negative statements:

*'Have you **ever** learnt to snowboard?'*
*'No, I haven't **ever** wanted to.'*

since and for

6 We often use the present perfect with ***since*** and ***for***. We use ***since*** with a time (e.g. ***six o'clock, last week***) and ***for*** with a period of time (e.g. ***three weeks, three hours***):

*Paul **has been** here **since** nine o'clock.*
*Jenny **has** only **been** here **for** about half an hour.*

2 Match the following present perfect examples with the appropriate explanations of use (2–4) on page 30. The first one is done for you.

a Ingrid has lived in Stockholm for six years. ......explanation 2......

b Janet has already been to New York three times this year. ....

c Peter has just bought a new car! He's selling the old one. ....

d I've forgotten how to write in Greek. ....

e Lucy has worked for the same company for over a year. ....

3 Complete the following sentences with the correct form of the verb in brackets and either *since* or *for*. The first one is done for you.

a Ashley (live) ...has lived... in a camper van ...for... three years.

b He (be) .... a writer .... October 1999.

c His wife, Stella, (work) .... on an organic farm ....Ashley gave up his job.

d They (not eat) .... any meat .... two years.

e Ashley (speak) .... French .... he was a child.

f They (be) .... married .... ten years.

g I (not see) .... them .... last January.

h He (have) .... a shaved head .... May last year.

4 Look at the pictures and ask a question about each one. The first one is done for you.

a ...Has he finished his meal?...

b ....

c ....

d ....

e ....

f ....

B Present perfect continuous

form and use

1 **Read the following explanations.**

present perfect continuous – form

1 We make the *present perfect continuous* by using the *auxiliary verb **has/have*** with the *past participle* ***been*** and the ***-ing*** form of the main verb:

*She **has been waiting** for him to ring all morning.*
*They **have been preparing** for the party all day.*
*Joanna and I **have been talking** for over an hour.*

In conversation we often contract the auxiliary to *'s/'ve*, particularly after pronouns (e.g. ***I***, ***she***, ***they***):

She's been waiting ... They've been preparing ...

present perfect continuous – use

2 We use the present perfect continuous to talk about something that began in the past and is still continuing:

*I've **been waiting** for the fridge to be delivered since four o'clock.*

3 We use the present perfect continuous to talk about something that has very recently finished, but that continued for some time:

*Felix **has been working out** at the gym.*

4 We often use the present perfect continuous with ***since*** and ***for***:

*Annette has been thinking about moving house **since** 1998.*
*She has been looking for a new house **for** about a year.*

5 We often use the present perfect continuous in questions with ***how long*** to ask how long something has been happening:

***How long** has Jane been working in Brussels?*

Remember: there are certain verbs that are not usually used in the continuous, including verbs describing feelings such as ***want, like, hate, hope etc.*** and other stative verbs such as ***remember, recognise, belong*** (see point 4 of Unit 1, Section A, Exercise 1).

2 **Read the descriptions in blue and write what you think has been happening. The first one is done for you.**

a Two boys are climbing out of a swimming pool.
The boys have been swimming.

b Mark is holding a cloth and a can of window cleaner and standing back from a shiny window.
....

c The ground is covered with snow. The sun is shining and the sky is clear.
....

d Tom has just come off the dance floor. He's absolutely exhausted.
....

e Jane is wearing oven gloves and carrying a steaming dish in each hand to the table.
....

f Mr and Mrs Thomas are walking into their home carrying carrier bags and boxes.
....

g Megan is standing in front of a painting – she is holding a paintbrush.
....

h My dog is covered in mud and he's standing in a hole in the garden.
....

3 Rewrite the sentences using the present perfect continuous and the word in brackets.

a Freda started learning Greek three years ago.
(for) ....

b I started watching TV at six o'clock. (since)
....

c John stopped and got out of his new car two minutes ago. (just)
....

d I started living on a houseboat six months ago – and I still do.
(for) ....

e Jane wasn't skating on the ice this morning. (just)
....

f The Gordon family go to Ireland every year. They started going there ten years ago. (for)
....

g Maria started listening to classical music when she was a child.
(since.) ....

h Keith has finished digging a new flower bed. (just)
....

i Phillip works in the City of London. He started there on 18th January. (since)
....

j Susan and Jack are talking about their relationship. They started three hours ago. (for)
....

4 Read the information about Rita and Tom Redfern and write questions for the answers. The first one is done for you.

Rita and Tom Redfern live in California, USA. Tom's a guitarist in a band called Moondance and Rita works for a recording company called Halcyon Music. Here are some facts about them.

- They moved to America a year ago.
- They bought their beach house last January.
- Rita started working for Halcyon Music last Monday.
- Tom started playing the guitar at the age of eight.
- Rita started her Japanese study classes six months ago.
- Tom joined a band called Moondance nine months ago.

a How long have they been living in America? For 12 months.
b ....? Since January.
c ....? Since Monday.
d ....? Since he was eight.
e ....? For six months.
f ....? For nine months.

C Mixed practice

present perfect simple and continuous

1 Read the sentences. Write the correct present perfect simple or continuous form in the gaps. Use the verbs in brackets. The first one is done for you.

a I (1 live) ..have lived.... in many strange places in my life and I (2 like) .... all of them – except for the houseboat! I lived in a houseboat which sank in the middle of the night. Luckily, I escaped but since then I (3 be) .... very suspicious of any kind of boat, and I (4 not/be able to) .... sleep very well at night, so I (5 never/want) .... to try a houseboat again.

b I (1 always want) ....to live at the top of a tall apartment block. I (2 live) .... in a basement flat for about four years, but since May I (3 look) .... for a penthouse.

c Bob (1 drive) .... thousands of miles in his old camper van over the years. He (2 repaired) .... it lots of times, but in the end he (3 have to) .... buy a new one. He (4 keep) .... the old one in the garage since 1999, but he (5 not/drive) .... it since then.

d FRANK: Hello Steve. What have you got in that bag?
STEVE: Hi Frank. I (1 fish) .... I (2 catch) .... six trout and a pike.
FRANK: Where (3 you/fish) ....?
STEVE: I (4 just/get back) .... from the lake out at Farmoor. I (5 try) .... lots of different places around here but I (6 never/be) .... this successful before.

2 Choose the correct word or phrase from the box to complete the following dialogue.

noticed
lost
haven't done
been working
ever tried
used
ever been
haven't
n't had
have found

IAN: Have you (**a**) .... karate?
DENNIS: No, I'm afraid I (**b**) ....
IAN: What about kick boxing?
DENNIS: No, I'm afraid I (**c**) .... that, either.
IAN: There is a martial arts centre round the corner. Have you (**d**) .... there? My girlfriend and I have (**e**) .... it lots of times.
DENNIS: No, I haven't (**f**) .... it. Anyway, recently I have (**g**) .... enough time to do that kind of thing. I've (**h**) .... very hard.
IAN: Yes, I know what you mean. Our jobs are very stressful, too, but we (**i**) .... it relaxing. You really should come too.
DENNIS: No thanks. I seem to have (**j**) .... my sports clothes. And actually I prefer to watch a video to relax.

3 Choose the appropriate word in the box to complete the following sentences. Some of the words are used more than once.

yet	since	again	so
for	already	always	

a Grace has been at college .... two terms now.

b She has made lots of friends ....

c She has .... joined the drama society.

d She hasn't managed to get a part in a play ....

e Her best friend Ursula has been studying at the college .... two years.

f Ursula and Grace have been sharing a room .... last term.

g Grace has .... been a good student ...

h and she has worked hard .... this term.

i Ursula hasn't been .... hard-working.

j She failed her last two exams, but she has been working very hard .... then.

4 Now look again at the last exercise and make questions about the girls' life at college. Use the answers given. The first one is done for you.

a 'How long has Grace been at college?'
'For two terms.'

b '....................'
'She's made lots.'

c '....................'
'Yes, she joined it last term.'

d '....................'
'No, unfortunately she hasn't got one yet.'

e '....................'
'For two years.'

f '....................'
'Since last term.'

g '....................'
'Yes, she always has.'

h '....................'
'Yes, this term too.'

i '....................'
'No, not as hard as Grace.'

j '....................'
'Yes, she has been working much harder.'

UNIT 6

A The passive

form and general use

1 Read this explanation of the passive.

passive – form

The *passive* is formed by adding a form of the *auxiliary* ***be*** to the *past participle* of the main verb.

- Present simple passive: *Stamps* ***are sold*** *in supermarkets now.*
- Present continuous passive: *Gabriel's room* ***is being painted*** *this afternoon.*
- Present perfect passive: *The CD* ***has been recorded*** *in London.*
- Past simple passive: *Jane* ***was*** *last* ***seen*** *in Paris.*
- Past continuous passive: *The cat* ***was being chased.***
- Future passive: *The doctor* ***will be given*** *an award in October.*

We form passive questions by putting the *auxiliary verb* ***be*** at the beginning of the sentence, or after the question word:

__Was__ the picture __painted__ by your sister?
Who __were__ the curtains __made__ by?

passive – use

When we don't know (or don't have any interest in) the agent of an action we can use a passive:

Some houses __were built.__

Note: We can often say the same thing with ***they*** + an active verb:

They built *some houses.*

In a passive sentence the important thing is what happens to the subject, and not who or what did it:

The little boy __is being kidnapped!__
I've __been robbed!__

2 Read the following information about the Great Pyramid and underline the passive verbs.

The Great Pyramid was built in Egypt about 5,000 years ago. It was constructed to the west of the River Nile. This area was called 'The land of the Dead'. The Great Pyramid was made from huge blocks of limestone. The wheel had not yet been invented, so the blocks of stone were pulled from the quarry by hundreds of men on a path of wooden logs. The pyramid was designed with a solid core of limestone with four sides, and gaps were left for corridors and various rooms. It is not known exactly what the pyramids were used for, but burial chambers (where the bodies of dead Pharaohs and their family and servants were placed) have been found deep inside the pyramids. It is thought that pyramids were designed to help the Pharaoh's spirit rise up to the sun after death. The pyramids are visited by millions of people each year.

3 Now read the following information about the famous ship the *Titanic* and write the correct passive form of the verb in brackets in each gap.

The *Titanic* (**a** build) .... in 1912. It (**b** design) .... in a new way and it (**c** think) .... to be unsinkable. Because of this, it (**d** not/give) .... enough lifeboats for the passengers and crew. The hull (**e** damage) .... by a collision with a huge iceberg and it sank very fast. A total of 1,513 people (**f** drown) .... that day. Because of this disaster, new international safety laws (**g** pass) .... and the Ice Patrol (**h** establish) .... In 1985 the wreck (**i** locate) .... on the sea bed and the ship (**j** explore) .... Several successful films (**k** make) .... about the Titanic since then, and the most recent (**l** released) .... in 1997.

4 Look at the pictures and write a suitable passive caption for each one using the verb in brackets. The first one is done for you.

a (hit) The boy has been hit by the ball.

b (build) ....

c (arrest) ....

d (give) ....

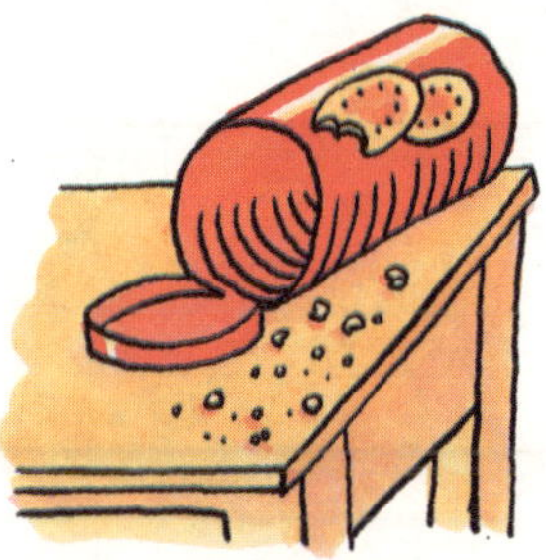

e (eat) ....

f (spill) ....

B Particular uses of the passive

passives used in technical and scientific writing; passive + *by* + agent; sentences with direct and an indirect object

1 Read the following explanations of how to use the passive.

using the passive

1 We use the *passive* when we do not know who the agent of the action is (or we do not want to say who it is):

*The freezer **was left** open all night.*

or, if the agent is known but not significant:

*My shoes **have been repaired.***

or, so that the subject of the verb is not a very long phrase:

*Tom was very impressed by **the way Derek managed the company.***

(Rather than: *The way Derek managed the company impressed Tom.*)

2 We frequently use the passive in scientific and technical writing:

*The results of the experiments **are** then **analysed** in the laboratory.*

3 We use the passive in historical and geographical texts:

*The pound **was devalued** in the 1960s.*
*The English king, Charles I, **was executed** in 1649.*

4 We often use the passive (particularly with modal verbs, e.g. ***can, must, should***) to express an instruction or rule in a courteous and impersonal way:

*It is important that this **is done** quickly.*
*The doors **must be kept** shut at all times.*
*Mobile phones **should be switched** off.*
*The answer **can be found** on page 6.*

using the passive with by

5 If you want to specify who or what the agent is in a passive sentence you use ***by*** after the *main verb* or the *object*:

*The trees **were blown down by** the storm.*
*My father **was left** a fortune **by** an uncle.*

6 We use this pattern when we want to indicate that the agent is particularly significant or unexpected:

*The last chocolate **was eaten by** Josephine (not by Mary).*

something was given to someone

7 Some sentences have a *direct* and an *indirect object*:

*They awarded **the Nobel Prize for Literature** to **Nadine Gordimer**.*

These sentences can be made passive in two different ways.

- They can start with the direct object (with ***to*** or ***for*** after the verb):

  *The Nobel Prize for Literature was awarded **to** Nadine Gordimer.*
  *A sweater was knitted **for** Paul by his mum.*

- They can start with the indirect object:

  Nadine Gordimer was awarded the Nobel Prize for Literature.
  Paul was knitted a sweater by his mum.

2 **Read the following texts and write down all the passive verbs you can find. Then decide why there are so many passive verbs in each text. Look at explanations 1–6 opposite, and write in the brackets which one applies to each paragraph. The first one is done for you.**

a Jean Baptiste Lamarck, who lived between 1744 and 1829, was a naturalist who was best known for his theory of evolution. His book on the theory of evolution, which was called *Philosophie Zoologique*, was published in 1809. Lamarck suggested that an organism changes throughout its lifetime, and these features are inherited by the next generation.

was known, was called, was published

are inherited [2]

b Meknes is one of the most beautiful and famous cities in Morocco. It was known as 'the Moroccan Versailles' because of its large and exotic palaces. They were built in the 17th century, in the reign of Mawlay Is'mail. Now it is used as a trading centre for agricultural products and valuable carpets.

.... [ ]

c When handling the product it is important that gloves are worn at all times. The product is corrosive and if it comes into direct contact with the skin or eyes, they must be washed immediately with large amounts of cold water. A mask should also be worn to prevent inhalation.

.... [ ]

d The internal combustion engine is an engine in which fuel is burnt inside the engine itself. The first one was patented in 1876, by N. Otto. It used gas as a fuel. It was the invention of the carburettor that enabled liquid fuel, particularly petrol, to be used.

.... [ ]

e The results of this year's Mainstream music awards have surprised everyone. In the Best Male Vocalist category the prize was won by James Kirk, not Lenny King, as expected. In the Best Group category, the award was given to East City Down, a band which nobody has heard of. The award for Best Dance Track was presented by the rapper Tootsie Cool, even though he doesn't like DJ Ice, the man who won it. But the biggest surprise was the Best Newcomer category where the gold statue was awarded to Eryl Krause even though she is 58.

.... [ ]

3 **Read explanation 7 opposite and then make two passive sentences from each of the following statements. The beginning of the first two sentences is given.**

a The chef baked a huge cake for the President's daughter.

A huge cake ....

The President's daughter ....

b The director of the gallery showed the journalists the new sculpture. ....

....

c A record company offered Robbie Williams a multi-million-dollar contract recently. ....

....

d The government granted some war veterans a pardon.

....

....

C Mixed practice

uses of the passive

1 **Look at the two pictures and write sentences about the differences between them, using the cues. The first one is done for you.**

BEFORE

AFTER

a The picture has been changed. (change)
b A rug .... (put)
c The ornaments .... (throw away)
d A large plant .... (put)
e The telephone .... (attach)
f The armchairs and sofa .... (take away)
g The carpet .... (take away)
h Blinds .... (install)
i The walls .... (paint)
j The lampshade .... (replace)

2 **Complete each gap with one of the following verbs. Decide if they should be active or passive. The first two are done for you.**

agree	knight
appoint	know
behead	make (x2)
change	release
convict	resign
die	start
educate	write
enter	summon
imprison	

A Man for All Seasons is a film that tells the story of Sir Thomas More.

Thomas More was born in London on 7 February 1478. He (a) was educated at the University of Oxford, and in 1504 he (b) entered Parliament. However, he spoke out against the king (Henry VII) and because of this More's father (c) .... He (d) (not) .... until Thomas More, his son, agreed to leave public life.

After Henry VII died and his son, Henry VIII, became king, More entered public life again. He (e) .... in 1521 which means he became 'Sir Thomas More'. He (f) .... speaker (chief official) of the House of Commons, England's parliament.

During this period, Sir Thomas More was close to the king. They frequently had long and enjoyable conversations and in 1529 Sir Thomas More (g) .... Lord Chancellor of England by his friend the king. The Lord Chancellor is the chief law official in the country.

Trouble (h) .... when Henry VIII wanted to divorce his first wife, Catherine of Aragon. More (i) (not) .... with this because of his religious beliefs and so (j) .... from public life (again) in 1532. But this was not enough for the king. He was desperate for More's approval. But Sir Thomas would not (**k**) .... his mind. The king was furious and, as a result, Sir Thomas More (**l**) .... to court and (**m**) .... of treason, a serious crime against the king and the state. He (**n**) .... on 7 July 1535. Four hundred years later, he (**o**) .... a saint by the Catholic church because he (**p**) .... for his beliefs.

Sir Thomas (**q**) (also) .... for his book *Utopia*, which (**r**) .... in 1516.

3 **Look at the phrases on the left and make a passive sentence. Start your sentence with the words in blue, and make the verb in brackets passive, as in the example. You may need to add *by* before the agent.**

a Millions of emails around the world every day (send) — *Millions of emails are sent around the world every day.*

b The *Mona Lisa* a few people every day (photograph) ....

c *Cats*, the musical more people than any other musical (see) ....

d Heathrow Airport more than 1.5 million people every year (use) ....

e The mountain, Machu Picchu 68,000 people since last January (visit) ....

f Mount Everest teams from all over the world every year (climb) ....

g The 'Vendée Globe' round-the-world yacht race a woman never (win) ....

h The Great Wall of China astronauts in space (see) ....

UNIT 7

A The future

present simple and present continuous as future

1 Read the following explanations of how the present simple and present continuous are used with future meaning.

present simple

1 We use the *present simple* for future schedules or timetables rather than personal plans:

The Bristol train ***leaves*** *at 8 am.*
The college term ***starts*** *in October.*

Note: there isn't a special future tense in English. Instead we use a number of different ways of talking about it. These include the present continuous and present simple (see above) and ***going to*** or ***will*** (see Section B).

present continuous

2 We use the *present continuous* to talk about personal plans and arrangements:

My aunt's ***coming*** *for tea this afternoon.*
Dr Wilson ***is speaking*** *at the conference this year.*

3 There are some verbs that are not usually used in the continuous, and this also applies to the future use of the present continuous. We do not usually use stative verbs such as ***be***, ***wait***, etc. in the continuous with future meaning. In these cases we usually use ***will***.

2 Now read the passage and look at the verbs in blue. Write down whether each one refers to the past, the present or the future.

Good morning everyone. I (**a**) am glad to announce that next Monday our President (**b**) is starting his tour of the factory. According to the itinerary his PA (**c**) sent us he (**d**) is spending three days with our company. (**e**) I'm sure we (**f**) are all very keen to make his visit a good one. On Monday morning his flight (**g**) lands at Stansted Airport at 9.15. Steve (**h**) is picking him up at the airport and (**i**) driving him to the main building. He (**j**) spends the first day talking to management and clerical staff. Miss Evans, (**k**) could you open the window please? Thank you. Now, where (**l**) was I? Oh yes … On Tuesday he (**m**) talks to factory floor workers and then, on Thursday, he (**n**) attends the meeting of the board of directors. He (**o**) is leaving on Friday and (**p**) flying to Dublin to visit our sister company there. Then, he (**q**) goes through the whole programme again.

....

....

....

....

....

....

3 Read the dialogue and underline the future form, in blue, that is better. In some cases both forms are possible, but one is better than the other.

a MARIA: What time does the show start/is the show starting?
b DEBBIE: I think the curtain is going up/goes up at 7.30.
c MARIA: Oh dear! Keith meets/is meeting us at 7.00. That doesn't leave/isn't leaving us much time to get the tickets.

d PAUL: They're sending/send the annual report tomorrow.
e HAMISH: Do they fax/Are they faxing it, or does it come/is it coming in the post?
f PAUL: They usually post it but I think John is coming/comes in the van tomorrow so he brings/is bringing it.

g HAIRDRESSER: So where do you go/are you going on holiday this year?
h CUSTOMER: Well I have/'m having two holidays, actually.
i HAIRDRESSER: Oh, you are lucky. I only am getting/get one week in the summer. I go/'m going to Barbados this year.

j TOUR GUIDE: Come on now, the coach leaves in five minutes. Where do you go/are you going, Mr Arkwright?
k MR ARKWRIGHT: According to the itinerary the coach is leaving/leaves at 3 p.m. We don't get/aren't getting to Paris until 7. I want another half-hour here.
l TOUR GUIDE: I'm sorry but there is a serious traffic jam. We are leaving/leave now with you or without you!

4 Use the words in brackets to make questions about the future, using the present simple or the present continuous. The first one is done for you.

a (where/you/go/this afternoon) '*Where are you going this afternoon*?' 'To the park with Jane.'
b (what/you/do this evening) '..........?' 'I've got a training session at the gym.'
c (when/film/start) '..........?' 'In half an hour.'
d (how/Kevin/get to the station) '..........?' 'By bus.'
e (what/be/on TV this evening) '..........?' 'A programme about the Liverpool football team.'
f (Jane/come/to see us with the new baby) '..........?' 'Yes, she'll be here at about 3.'
g (when/you/go/to the supermarket) '..........?' 'I was thinking of tomorrow morning.'
h (when/the meteorite/pass close to the earth) '..........?' 'About midnight, the paper says.'
i (how/he/get in touch with you) '..........?' 'On his mobile phone, I should think.'
j (you/put/sugar in that) '..........?' 'No. I prefer it without sugar.'

B The future

be going to + infinitive; *will* + infinitive

1 Read these explanations of how we use *be going* to and *will* with future meaning.

be going to

1 We use ***be going to*** + *infinitive* when we talk about something that, on current evidence, seems almost inevitable:

*I'm sure **it's going to rain**. Look at the sky!*
*Kevin **is going to fail** the maths exam. He hasn't attended any of the classes.*

2 We also use ***be going to*** + *infinitive* when we are talking about something someone intends to happen, particularly where the intention is strong:

*Rosa **is going to learn** to drive if she possibly can.*
***I'm going to finish** the marathon if it kills me!*

Note: If we want to use an *adverb*, such as ***probably*** or ***definitely***, it goes after the auxiliary verb:

*She's **probably** going to be late.*
*The advanced students are **definitely** going to pass the exam.*

will

3 We use ***will*** + *infinitive* as a statement of future fact, or to say what we think will happen:

*It'**ll be** summer soon.*
*She'**ll** probably **pass** the exam.*

4 We use ***will*** + *infinitive* when there is some form of condition, either stated or implied:

*I'**ll buy** a new dress **if** he invites me to the theatre.*
*We'**ll get on** the bus **when** it comes.*

5 We use ***will*** + *infinitive* when we are offering to do something:

*I'**ll finish** laying the table, if you like.*

or, when we are promising something:

*John **will help** you while I'm out, don't worry.*

or, when we are asking someone to do something:

***Will you pass** me that pen, please?*

Let's; should; shall

6 When we are suggesting doing something in the future we use ***Let's***, ***Why don't you***, or ***should/must*** + *infinitive*:

*Come on, **let's go** and see your new flat.*
***Why don't you come** too?*
*Jack **should take** some time off work.*

7 We use ***shall*** instead of ***will*** in questions with ***I*** and ***we***:

***Shall** we **get** some coffee?*
***Shall** I **try** to find the right bus for you?*

Shall can be used in affirmative sentences, but it is quite old-fashioned and it is not very common in speech:

*I **shall** always **remember** that evening!*
*We **shall drive** down to Madrid this year.*

Note: although there are some situations where there is only one correct form of the future, there are many situations where it is possible to use either ***going to*** or ***will*** (or the present continuous). People choose the one that sounds best.

2 **Complete these sentences about the picture using the words in the box. The first one is done for you.**

arrest	get into	play	steal	thief
buy	guitar	rain	take	tree
climb	newspaper	see	taxi	wallet
film	photograph			

a The man with glasses is going to buy a newspaper.
b A woman in a yellow suit ....
c The people in the queue ....
d The tourist in shorts ....
e The little boy ....
f The man with a beard ....
g The police officer ....
h The boy with the red T-shirt ....
i Look at those clouds! It ....

3 **Some of the future verbs in these sentences are not the best choice. Put a line through the words that are wrong and write the correct verb on the line, or write correct if there is no problem.**

a Shall James try to mend the bicycle? ....
b Delia will bring us some French jam if she can. ....
c Let you give me the salt, please. ....
d I hope the new series of Trash is going to begin in the autumn. ....
....
e He says he's going to post the book to me today. ....
f Sarah will have her baby next week. ....
g I promise I'm going to visit her in the hospital. ....
h Do you think Phil is going to be famous one day? ....

4 **Look at all these sentences with *will* and *shall*. Decide whether the sentences are *Requests*, *Offers* or *Promises*. Write R, O or P in the brackets.**

a Shall I help you carry your luggage? [ ]
b I'll bring a trolley next time. [ ]
c Will you move your bag a bit? I can't get through. [ ]
d I'll find us a seat in a quiet carriage if you like. [ ]
e Louis will give you some money when we get back. [ ]
f Shall we buy you a present from London? [ ]
g Will you ask the guard why we are so delayed? [ ]
h We'll be there in a few minutes! [ ]
i If you want, I'll get you a cup of coffee from the buffet. [ ]
j Will you come with us to the theatre this evening? [ ]
k I'll never do this journey again! [ ]

C Mixed practice

present simple and present continuous; *will* and *be going to*

1 Look at the following sentences. Underline the future verbs and write down the number of the explanation from sections A and B that each one demonstrates.

a We are going to see a film tonight. explanation B2
b I don't feel very well. I think I'm going to faint. ....
c We're meeting them outside the cinema at eight. ....
d If I can afford it, I think I'll visit my sister in Mexico next summer. ....
e According to the weather forecast it is going to rain later on today. ....
f Sit down and relax. I'll make you a nice cup of tea. ....
g According to the guide book the museum closes today at 4.30. ....
h Who's going to give her the bad news? I don't have the nerve. ....
i Why don't you come with me? ....
j Shall I phone the airport to check the flight? ....
k If we don't hurry up, we'll miss the train. ....
l He'll leave school next year. ....
m I'll probably never see you again! ....

2 Read the following sentences and choose which phrase is better in the second sentence and underline it. The first one is done for you.

a The newspaper says it's going to snow.
It's probably going to snow./It's probably snowing.
b I have an appointment at the hairdresser tomorrow at 3.
I'm going to the hairdresser tomorrow./I go to the hairdresser tomorrow.
c Mark is feeling very dizzy.
He faints./He's going to faint.
d If the sail hits the water …
… the boat will turn over./the boat is turning over.
e I'm hungry. Come on, …
… we have a sandwich./let's have a sandwich.
f They've offered Penny a place at Bristol University!
The course is going to start in October./The course starts in October.
g Yvonne and Frank are playing chess this afternoon.
Frank is definitely going to win./Frank is definitely winning.
h I know!
I buy you a watch for your birthday!/I'll buy you a watch for your birthday!
i I can't quite reach that box of tissues on the top shelf.
Will you pass them to me, please?/Are you going to pass them to me, please?

3 **Choose the most appropriate verb form (*will*, *be going to*, present continuous or present simple) for the words in brackets in this conversation. The first one is done for you.**

HELENA: (**a** we/be) ...Are we going to be... in time?

SUSIE: Yes, I think so.

HELENA: What time (**b** the train/arrive) ....?

SUSIE: At 8.15. Oh no, wait a minute, look, there's a delay. It (**c** not/get in) ....until nine o'clock.

HELENA: What (**d** we/do) .... until then?

SUSIE: I don't know.

HELENA: Well I (**e** get) .... a coffee. Do you want one?

SUSIE: No, but I (**f** come) .... to the cafeteria with you.

HELENA: What (**g** you/say) .... to him when you see him?

SUSIE: I don't really know. I mean I can't think of anything to say.

HELENA: Don't worry. I (**h** do) .... the talking.

SUSIE: OK. I (**i** just/stand) .... and listen.

HELENA: I don't believe that for a moment.

SUSIE: Well I (**j** not/shout) .... at him or anything. Just because he said he'd catch an earlier train. I mean he's nearly 17.

HELENA: What (**k** he/do) .... when he leaves school?

SUSIE: I wish I knew. He (**l** probably/go) .... travelling with his friends. That's what they all seem to do.

HELENA: (**m** you/miss) .... him?

SUSIE: Yes, I think so. It (**n** feel) .... very strange with no one in the house except for me and the dog.

SUSIE: Oh dear. This cafeteria (**o** close) .... in five minutes.

HELENA: Then we (**p** wait) .... on the platform. Stop worrying.

SUSIE: I just hope he (**q** be) .... on the train!

UNIT 8

A Present modals (1)

recommendation and obligation

1 Read the following explanation of the use of modal verbs.

introduction

1 *Modal* verbs are verbs that have the same form for all persons (e.g. ***I***, ***you he***, ***she***). We can use them to say whether something is necessary or is a good idea, and to say how certain or possible something is. They modify the meaning of the verb that follows.

form

2 Modals (e.g. ***must***, ***should***, ***may***) are *auxiliary* verbs and are followed by an *infinitive*. We don't need to add ***do*** or ***don't*** when we make questions or negative sentences:

*You **mustn't talk** in an exam.*
***Should** we **sign** the paper now?*

Note: when we answer a question using a short answer we repeat the modal verb: *'Should we turn over the paper now?' 'Yes, you **should**.' 'Might the car break down?' 'Yes, I think it **might**.'*

3 ***Need to*** and ***have to*** are semi-modals and so we must use an auxiliary with them:

*Jane **doesn't need to** get a new permit.*
***Will** we **have to** pay again?*

Note: Compare ***need to*** and ***need***. We do not add ***don't*** to ***need*** when we make a negative sentence:

*Jane **needn't get** a new permit.*

obligation

4 In order to express *obligation* (that is, something we are obliged to do because it is the law or a rule or an individual forces us to) we use ***must***, ***need to*** and ***have to*** or ***have got to***:

*You **must get to work** by 8.30.*
*You **need to wear** the right clothes.*
*You **have to use** the key code to get into the building.*
*You've **got to leave the** building if you hear the fire alarm.*

Note: When we are expressing our own opinion and not a general rule or law we usually say ***must***:

*You **must hurry**! It's going to rain.*

5 To say that it is obligatory not to do something we use ***must not*** (***mustn't***):

*Customers **must not** bring pets into the shop.*

6 To say that something is not compulsory we use ***need not***, ***don't need to*** or ***don't have to***.

*The employees **need not** stay until 6 o'clock.*
*They **needn't arrive** until 9 a.m.*
*We **don't have to work** at the weekend.*

recommendation

7 To recommend doing something because it is better or right we use ***had better***, ***ought to*** or ***should***:

*We'**d better get to** the cinema early.*
*You **ought to** invite your sister.*
*We **should buy** our tickets in advance.*

8 To say that something is not recommended we say ***ought not to*** or ***should not***, or ***had better not***:

*You **oughtn't to** stay up so late.*
*We **shouldn't** eat so much salt.*
*You'**d better not** forget my birthday!*

2 Read the following text and underline the verbs that are expressing an obligation or a recommendation, according to the explanations on page 48. List all the verbs and write the number of the appropriate explanation from Exercise 1 beside them. There are 14 verbs. The first one is done for you.

Leanne really needs to get fit. She decided to get a personal trainer. He told her she ought to lose a few pounds and she should improve her fitness. To do that she has to go to the gym three times a week. She mustn't let herself get dehydrated, so she has to drink 2 litres of water a day. She doesn't have to buy special equipment, but she mustn't wear tight clothing. She should, however, have good-quality shoes. She needn't cut out all her favourite foods, but she must eat a sensible balanced diet. While she is exercising she shouldn't let herself get too tired. Her husband thinks she shouldn't spend so much time at the gym, but she says she hopes she doesn't have to give it up now, she's feeling so great!

a needs to get – explanation 4
b ...
c ...
d ...
e ...
f ...
g ...
h ...
i ...
j ...
k ...
l ...
m ...
n ...

3 Circle the verb in blue that is the most appropriate verb in these sentences.

a Doctors have to/ought to work very long hours.

b In many countries people should/have to wear seat belts in the back of cars as well as in the front.

c You needn't/mustn't get up early if you don't want to.

d You shouldn't/mustn't use your mobile phone in here. I mean it's not against the law but it's a bit anti-social.

e You'd better not/don't have to wear a helmet when you are on your bicycle. It's your choice.

f You don't have to/ought not to play loud music. It upsets the neighbours.

g I think I'm getting fat. I hope I don't have to/shouldn't cut out chocolate.

h Bob ought not to/doesn't need to go to work since he won the lottery.

4 Use the modal verbs in brackets to make sentences from the following words. Be careful when you have to make a question or a negative. The first one is done for you.

a I/eat/my sandwich outside? (must)
Must I eat my sandwich outside?

b I/get/here before 7 o'clock? (should)
...

c you/have/identification to take books out of the library? (need to) ...

d you/worry/about the washing up. (need not)
...

e they/hurry up/the concert starts in ten minutes. (should) ...

f she/take/the science exam? (have to) ...

g they/spray-paint/any more walls. (had better not) ...

h we/wear/smart clothes for your party? (need)
...

B Present modals (2)

possibility, ability, permission

1 **Read the following explanation of how we express possibility, ability and permission with modals.**

possibility

1 We use the modals ***may*** and ***might*** with the *infinitive* of a *stative* verb to say that something is possibly the case now or in the future:

*You **may think** this is true.*
*John **might wish** he had a car like mine.*

2 We use the modals ***may*** and ***might*** with ***be*** and an ***-ing*** form of an active verb to show that we think something is possibly happening in the present:

*Jack **may be working** in the shop today.*
*The company **might be manufacturing** a new model at the moment.*

3 We use ***may*** and ***might*** with a future meaning with the *infinitive* of an active verb:

*Ursula **may arrive** this afternoon.*
*She **might bring** David with her.*

ability

4 We use ***can*** to say that we think someone is able to do something in the present:

*Lucy **can dance** really well.*

We use ***can't*** when someone is not able to do something:

*Keith **can't dance** at all.*

5 If we are speaking politely, we use ***could*** or ***couldn't*** to talk about ability and possibility:

*I think I **could reach** that book.*
*It **could be** worse.*

Or when we want to request or suggest things:

***Could** you **lend** me five pounds?*
*We **could take** a taxi.*

6 We use ***be able to*** to express ability when we are writing or speaking in a formal way:

*The managing director **is able to make** a decision unilaterally.*
*We **are** also **able to offer** the product at a reduced price.*

permission

7 We use ***can*** when something is permitted:

*You **can** eat your packed lunch in the canteen.*

We also use ***can*** and ***can't*** to ask if something is permitted or not permitted:

***Can** I **pay** by credit card?*
***Can't** you **buy** your ticket on the plane?*

8 We use ***can't*** to say when something is not permitted:

*You **can't smoke** in the train.*
*Sarah **can't use** my travel pass.*

9 We also use ***may*** for permission when we are speaking formally, especially in questions:

***May** I **take** another sandwich?*
*Students **may not enter** the room during the demonstration.*

2 Read the following conversation and write the number of the explanation that is relevant to the verbs in blue in each one. The first one is done for you.

a JANE: Can you remember what Mr Gross said to you? explanation 4

b TOM: Yes. He said 'I may not finish the project today'. He was very upset. ....

c JANE: Why can't he complete it today? ....

d TOM: I don't know. He may be too busy with other work. ....

e JANE: What help could I give? ....

f TOM: You might send him the sales figures from last month. ....

g JANE: No I can't! I've got to finish this filing for Helen! ....

h TOM: She might let you do that later. This is important. ....

i JANE: Helen isn't here at the moment, so I can't ask her. She might be working at home today. ....

j TOM: Well, I might have time to do the filing this afternoon. ....

k JANE: Can I send him a fax with the information he wants? ....

l TOM: I think Donald may be using the fax machine at the moment. ....

m JANE: Could you pass me the Janssen file? Thanks. ....

n TOM: Mr Gross is working too hard. I think he might be going crazy! ....

3 Choose which word in the box can be used in both the gaps in the following pairs of sentences.

can't
could
may
might
can

a 'I think she .... be late.' 'Yes, she .... not know the way.

b '.......... I bring the children in here?' 'Yes, of course. You .... take them into the family room.'

c '.......... I try some of this pie?' 'Yes, of course, but you .... not like it.'

d '.......... you move a little to the left? I want to take a picture.'
'Oh sorry. I .... take one of you, if you like.'

e '.......... I use my walkman in here?' 'No, I'm afraid you ....'

f 'I'm afraid I .... email you because I .... use my computer at the moment. Sorry.'

C Mixed practice

present modals

1 Sangita is 17. Complete these sentences about her using the right modals. The first one is done for you.

What do her teachers say to her?

a You ...should... work harder.

b You .... try to get to school on time.

c You .... wear so much make-up.

d You .... to do gym at the moment because you have exams.

What are the laws of England?

e She .... vote until she's 18.

f She .... go to 18-certificate films.

g She .... get a driving licence now that she's 17.

h She .... get married, with her parents' consent.

What does her mother say to her?

i Sangita! Come here! You .... do your homework before you go out!

j Your father says you .... play your music so loud.

k You .... tidy your room every day.

l But you .... tidy it sometimes!

2 Rewrite the following sentences using *should/ought to*, *must*, *have to*, *don't need/have to*, *can't*, or *had better*. Start each sentence with *You*.

a Getting up early isn't necessary tomorrow.

....

b Wearing a uniform is not compulsory at this school.

....

c Driving along this road is not permitted.

....

d Wearing a uniform is obligatory in this job.

....

e Retiring at 65 is obligatory in some companies.

....

f Going to see the doctor would be a really good idea, I think.

....

g Tell me if you are going to be late. I insist.

....

3 Rewrite the phrases in blue in better English, using one of the following verbs: *can*, *could*, *may*, *might*, *be able* to. Remember that sometimes more than one verb may be correct.

(a) It is possible that Harry is going to Chicago in June. At the moment, he has quite a lot of money saved and (b) he is able to buy a ticket. (c) He will possibly go with his friend Gordon. Gordon said to his boss, (d) 'Will you permit me to have a week off work in June?' His boss replied (e) 'You are permitted to have a week's holiday in June, but (f) please ask me a bit sooner next time. It's already May! Fortunately, (g) I am able to find someone to take your place as it is the university vacation and a lot of students (h) are able to work for me for a week.' Harry and Gordon are worried that (i) it is possible that it is too late to get cheap tickets. Harry phoned the travel agents and said, (j) 'Will you permit me to buy off-season tickets in May?' They said, (k) 'You are able to if you are travelling within one month.' So he booked his ticket straight away. Now Gordon has to book his ticket quickly because (l) he is able to have the reduced fare only if he books today. Harry thinks that Gordon (m) is possibly booking the ticket right now. If he isn't, (n) it is possible that he won't be able to go with his friend.

a ....
b ....
c ....
d ....
e ....
f ....
g ....
h ....
i ....
j ....
k ....
l ....
m ....
n ....

4 Look at the rules for the new reference library in Charleton. Make one sentence for each rule, using a modal or semi-modal verb. Start each sentence with *You*.

a ....
b ....
c ....
d ....
e ....
f ....
g ....
h ....
i ....
j ....

CHARLETON REFERENCE LIBRARY

LIBRARY RULES

Leave coats and umbrellas at the entrance.
No eating in the library.
No drinking in the library.
Silence at all times.
It is important that clothing is decent.
It is not necessary to ask before you take a book from the shelves.
Replace books when you've finished with them.
No books to be taken out of the library.
Catalogues are available for the readers.
Photocopying of documents is free.

UNIT 9

A Noun phrases
nouns with adjectives; nouns and prepositional phrases

1 **Read the explanations of how we use adjectives and prepositional phrases with nouns.**

noun phrases

1 We can modify or change the meaning of *nouns* by adding words before them. They can be adjectives:

*the **old** man*
*three **new** books*
***facial** expressions*

Or they can be nouns:

***body** language*
*a **door** handle*

2 We can also modify nouns by adding a phrase that starts with a preposition (e.g. ***with***, ***in***, ***on***, ***without***) after them:

*the house **at the end of the street***
*the apartment **by the river***

Note: We use ***with*** to add something special about a person or thing:

*a house **with** a tall chimney*
*a girl **with** long hair*

When we use the *definite article* ***the*** before the noun we often use ***the*** after the preposition:

***the** child **in the** blue coat*
***the** book **with the** red cover*

2 **Find the words or phrases in the box that could be used to modify the nouns in blue in the following sentences. Write them down in the correct order. The first one is done for you.**

at the side of the building
membership
temporary
without a card
at the desk
valuable
in the blue uniform
horrible
sports
dangerous

a The man stopped Jenny as she went into the club.
the man in the blue uniform

b 'Have you got your card?' he said.
....

c Jenny looked in her bag, but she couldn't find it.
....

d 'I'm afraid I can't let anyone into the club,' he said.
....

e Somebody has damaged a lot of equipment.
....

f 'But you know it wasn't me! I'm not a criminal!' she said.
....

g 'Well, you can get a card from the desk,' he said, smiling.
....

h 'Thank you, she said, 'the girl will recognise me, I'm sure.'
....

i Jenny followed the man through a door.
....

j 'Why would anyone do such a thing?' she wondered.
....

3 **Look at the picture and find the things listed below (a–j). Then fill in the gaps with an appropriate word before and a prepositional phrase after the first noun. The first one is done for you.**

a The ....rose.... garden ..behind.. the fence is beautiful.

b The .... car .... the car park belongs to Dr Jones.

c Can you see the .... man .... the tree?

d The .... balloon .... the sky is flying away.

e I'd like to own the .... house .... the left.

f The woman is afraid of the .... dog .... the man's legs.

g The .... boy .... the window is watching the balloon.

h An .... woman .... a basket of roses is walking down the path.

i The .... woman .... the tall man is his wife.

j The .... cat .... the car is afraid of the dog too.

4 **Match the phrases in the two columns to make sentences. The first one is done for you.**

a It's more expensive if you want a hotel → 6

b I need to buy a car

c They are building a new mosque

d Do you know that song *Lady*

e I'm waiting for the man

f Did you enjoy *Men*

g David Hockney is one of the most successful painters

h Have you got the latest book

i I really don't like the design

j In Sergio Leone's films there are usually a lot of men

k In Madrid there is a wonderful portrait

1 of the King of Spain.

2 from the vehicle recovery service. My car's broken down.

3 *in red*?

4 at the end of my street.

5 on the cover of that book.

6 near the seafront.

7 *in Black*?

8 with beards.

9 with a big engine and a large boot.

10 of his generation.

11 by J.K. Rowling?

B Describing nouns nouns followed by present and past participles

1 Read the explanations of how we describe nouns using present and past participles.

nouns with participle phrases

1 Look at these two sentences:

Sam owns that dog. The dog is scratching its ear.

We can make these two sentences into one sentence by adding a *present participle* (***-ing** form*) to the noun (shown in blue):

*Sam owns that dog **scratching** its ear.*

Note that the ***-ing** form* has an active meaning (see Unit 6, Section A):

*He spoke to the woman **sitting** next to him.* (She is sitting next to him.)

2 Look at these two sentences:

They heard some music. The music was composed by Villa-Lobos.

We can make these two sentences into one sentence by adding a *past participle* (***-ed** form*) to the noun (shown in blue) and a *preposition* (***by**, **in**, **on**, etc.*):

*They heard some music **composed by** Villa-Lobos.*

Note that the ***-ed*** form has a passive meaning (see Unit 6, Section A):

*The food **served on** the silver platter was delicious.* (The food was served.)

2 Complete these descriptions of some family photographs, using either a present or past participle of the verb in brackets in the gap.

a The small boy .... (lean) on the chair next to my grandmother is my father.

b This is the first photo .... (take) by my sister.

c The boy .... (hold) the cat is my cousin James.

d That's my sister sitting on the car .... (own) by my father at the time.

e The lady .... (sit) in the chair is my grandmother.

f This is the pony .... (give) to me by my mother when I was 10.

g This girl .... (get) married is my sister Karen.

3 **Complete the following news stories by adding the information in the boxes. Use either the present participle or the past participle after the noun.**

The report was published in the Daily Herald.
Cox and Proscutin constructed the bridge.
People were walking across it.
Martyn Jackson is employed by the City Council
The public have experienced problems.

The people were driving along the motorway.
The elephant was covered in ribbons and sequins.
The pagoda was brought from Manchester.
The gallery was opened by the mayor this morning.

The police squad are trained in surveillance.
The gang was seen on the security video.
The head of the city's crime division spoke on the television yesterday.
Anyone who sees the criminals should not approach them.

a A report (1) .... has said that the steel bridge (2) .... is unsafe. People (3) .... have felt it swaying from side to side. Martyn Jackson, the architect (4) ...., blames the construction company for the problems (5) ....

b People (1) .... were surprised to see a huge plastic elephant (2) .... It stood beside a 20-foot-high pagoda (3) .... They were intended to advertise the new art gallery (4) ....

c A special police squad (1) .... have been hunting the gang (2) .... The head of the city's crime division, (3) ...., warned that these men could be dangerous and that anyone (4) .... should not approach them. They should contact the police immediately.

4 **Read the following sentences and add a present or past participle from the box to complete the description. The first one is done for you.**

taught
covered
opening
sitting
created
hurrying
found
produced
trained
flowing

a She's a dancer ....trained.... in the USSR.
b Geography was the subject .... by my favourite teacher, Miss Webster.
c He told me about a new café .... in Trent Street tomorrow.
d Huckleberry Finn is the most famous character .... by Mark Twain.
e I've got one of the best cars .... by that company.
f That's the poor little boy .... in the subway.
g She followed the tall man .... down the hill.
h The policeman found a shirt .... in blood.
i The Seine is the name of the river .... through Paris.
j The woman pointed to the man .... in the corner.

C Mixed practice

nouns with adjectives, prepositional phrases, present participles, past participles

1 Read the following passage. Look at the nouns in blue and write down all the words and phrases that describe them. Two are done for you.

We went to a lovely (a) party last (b) night. It was given by the old (c) man from number 27. We really enjoyed the (d) meal cooked by his eldest son.

We then moved into the elegant (e) sitting room. It had blue (f) walls covered with expensive (g) paintings. Suddenly, there was a knock at the front (h) door. The (i) neighbour from number 29 went to answer it, but when she opened the old green (j) door, two (k) men wearing masks ran past her and came into the room.

It was terrifying. One of the men was carrying a (l) shotgun with two long (m) barrels, and he told us he'd kill us immediately if we moved a muscle. So we just sat there as they took the biggest (n) paintings in the house and wrapped them in a large (o) piece of white cloth. Then they ran out and got into a (p)van parked in front of the house.

We rang the police and two young (q) officers arrived in two minutes from the local (r) police station. They asked us long and detailed (s) questions. The tall (t) policeman with the big moustache told us they would do everything they could to catch the thieves.

a ....
b ....
c old, from number 27
d ....
e ....
f ....
g ....
h ....
i ....
j ....
k ....
l ....
m ....
n ....
o ....
p ....
q ....
r ....
s ....
t ....

2 Write sentences using the phrases in brackets to describe the nouns in blue in each sentence. You may have to add some words, and choose the right form of the verb. The first one is done for you.

a I like pictures of people (interesting faces)
I like pictures of people with interesting faces.

b Steve has three suits (expensive/design (v)/by Armani)
....

c I used to live in a(n) apartment (large/centre of town)
....

d When you are driving in the snow, you have to be careful of cars (skid (v)/on the ice) ....

e In London tourists often take photographs of soldiers (wear/red uniforms/black 'busby' hats) ....

f I've just bought a(n) edition of a book (first/write/Steve McCormack) ....

3 **Match the first and second half of each headline. The first one is done for you.**

a	Government closes cancer	1	... written by son	a	3
b	Father attacks book	2	... parked outside embassy	b	
c	Lawyer defends politician	3	... ward in local hospital	c	
d	Mother searches for son	4	... bitten by dog	d	
e	Photographer films woman	5	... sleeping in class	e	
f	Police blow up car	6	... accused of taking money	f	
g	Swimmer frees dolphin	7	... with memory loss	g	
h	Thieves steal picture	8	... accused of shoplifting	h	
i	Teachers find more pupils	9	... painted by Rembrandt	i	
j	Ambulance crew helps boy	10	... caught in net	j	

4 **Correct the following sentences, and explain why they are wrong. The first is done for you.**

a The house stands in a bordered by trees road.
The house stands in a road bordered by trees. (The past participle should go after the noun.)

b A very small bird yellow flew in through the window.

c I was amazed to see that the waving at me man was my father

d *Star Wars* was made by an enormous team of people creative.

e You should never shout at behaving badly children.

f I like my bread garlic dripping with butter.

g Mr Keithley loves all the written by Shakespeare plays.

h His wife owned a large Chevrolet old-fashioned.

i I support the playing in red team.

j Michael had a long nose pointed and short hair.

A Relative clauses (1)

defining relative clauses

1 Read the following explanations of defining relative clauses.

relative clauses and relative pronouns

1 Some sentences have just one *clause*:

He shouted at the computer.

But some have two or more clauses:

main clause	second clause
He shouted at the computer	*that had just stopped working.*

We call the second clause a *relative clause*. Relative clauses give us more information about the person or thing in the main clause. Look at the following sentences:

Mark was a dancer. He danced with the Royal Ballet.

You can put the two sentences together by making the second sentence a relative clause, and adding **who**:

*Mark was a dancer **who** danced with the Royal Ballet.*

2 In the examples above, ***who*** and ***that*** are *subject pronouns*. ***Who*** is a *subject pronoun* because it is the subject of the clause *... danced with the Royal Ballet*. ***That*** is a subject pronoun because it is the subject of the clause ... *had just stopped working*.

In the following sentence, however, ***that*** is an *object pronoun* because it refers to ***the car***, which is the object of the second clause:

*I bought the car **that** Mary was selling.*

(The second clause means 'Mary was selling **the car**'.)

defining relative clauses

3 When the second clause in a sentence identifies the noun in the first clause (by explaining who or what we are talking about) we call it a *defining* relative clause.

*Harry is the singer **who won that talent competition.***

The defining relative clause (***who won that talent competition***) has told us which singer Harry is.

form and use

4 To join a main clause to a relative clause we usually need to add a relative pronoun, such as ***who***, ***that***, ***which***, ***where***, ***when*** or ***why***.

- We use ***who*** for people, and for animals that we think of as nearly human:

  *Keith is the man **who** married Emily.*

  *That's the dog **who** ate all the biscuits off the plate!*

- We can also use ***that*** for people, but it is less common and slightly less formal:

  *Mary is the woman **that** sits next to me in class.*

- We use ***which*** or ***that*** for things:

  *Chocolate is the food **which** most people love best.*

  *That's the dog **that** I saw in my garden.*

- We also use the pronouns ***when*** and ***where*** for time and place:

  *That was the moment **when** I realised it was too late.*

  *Felicity went into the room **where** Bob was sitting.*

- When we are talking about something belonging to someone we use ***whose***:

  *I didn't really like the teacher **whose** class I used to attend.*

5 We can leave out the *object pronoun* (see explanation 2 opposite) in defining relative clauses

The woman (who) I saw in the supermarket is Paul's sister.

I bought a copy of the book (that) John wrote.

But this is not possible with subject pronouns:

*The man **who** interviewed me was very polite.*

NOT: ~~*The man interviewed me was very polite*~~.

6 We often use a relative clause in the middle of a sentence with the most important information at the end:

*The painting **which Sue hung in the hall** is a reproduction.*

*The meat **that Pete left in the fridge** is completely rotten.*

2 **Put the correct pronoun (*that*, *which*, *who*, *whose*, *when* or *where*) in the gaps in the following sentences.**

a He's the man .... won the lottery.
b That's the dog .... chased me in the park.
c Shall we buy the sofa .... we saw in the window yesterday?
d The village .... Alain lived is in Normandy.
e Everyone celebrated that day .... the agreement was signed.
f The café .... has internet access is on George Street.
g Who is the person .... ordered the pizza?
h Which is the street .... the museum is?
i The book .... has a yellow cover is a murder mystery.
j The woman .... basement was flooded has left the area.

3 **Look at explanation 5 above. Are the following sentences correct? If they are, put a tick (✓) in the brackets and, if not, a cross (✗). If you think you need to add a pronoun, which pronoun would you add?**

a Jason's the man Corinne married. (.....) ....
b He's the man met her at the golf course. (.....) ....
c They're the people invited us to their wedding. (.....) ....
d They're the family we have known for longest. (.....) ....
e He bought her the ring was lost later. (.....) ....
f That's the ring he gave her. (.....) ....
g His mother was the one cried all the time. (.....) ....
h This is a picture of a wedding happened last week. (.....) ....

4 **Choose a relative pronoun and a defining relative clause from the boxes, and then write them in the correct gap in the story. The first one is done for you.**

which who whose that

had once been his girlfriend
he had ever seen
he thought she would hate
she had given him all those years ago
invented this stupid machine
is electronically sensitive
meant that nobody had to fill in tickets any more
served him

Giles was very excited. He had been invited out by someone (a) who had once been his girlfriend. Giles wanted to wear the jacket (b) .... so he took it to the dry cleaners. When he got there the sales assistant (c) .... explained the computer system. She was especially enthusiastic about the recording system (d) .... 'You see,' she said, 'you just give me that jacket, and I put it in this basket (e) .... What do you think?' Giles was amazed. It was the most impressive thing (f) .... But when he went back to the dry cleaners two days later, the sales assistant couldn't find his jacket even though she searched for it for hours. 'What about the new system?' Giles protested. 'I can't help that,' she said, 'I'm not the person (g) ....' There was nothing that Giles could do. He went to the restaurant in an old jacket (h) .... When he walked in, his friend introduced him to her new husband.

B Relative clauses (2)

non-defining relative clauses

1 Read this explanation of non-defining relative clauses.

form and use

1 Non-defining relative clauses do not have to identify a *subject* because we already know what it is. Instead they give us more information about it. Look at these sentences:
Jack is in hospital at the moment. Jack is 65.
We can put these two sentences together using a *subject pronoun*, ***who***:
*Jack, **who** is 65, is in hospital at the moment.*
Notice that the non-defining relative clause often goes in the middle of the main clause.

2 Now look at these two sentences:
The lady next door phoned me today. I have never spoken to her before.
To put these together we need to add an *object pronoun*, ***who***. It refers to the object (***her***) of the verb (***have spoken to***) in the second sentence, which becomes the relative clause:
*The lady next door, **who** I have never spoken to before, phoned me today.*

3 Notice that you can't leave out the object pronoun before non-defining relative clauses:
*I served them all a meal, **which** they ate very fast.* → NOT: ~~*I served them all a meal they ate very fast*~~.

4 Notice the punctuation in non-defining relative clauses. We need to use a comma before and often after the clause.

5 The pronoun in a non-defining relative clause can sometimes refer to the whole of the main clause:
*Wilfred sent a dozen red roses, **which** was very generous of him.*
In this sentence ***which*** refers to ***sending a dozen roses***.

6 We use ***who*** for people, and ***which*** or ***that*** for things. (In non-defining clauses, we don't use ***that*** for people.) We also use ***when*** and ***where*** for time and place:
*Tom has rented a cottage in Charlbury, **where** he used to live.*
*She lived in the Dark Ages, **when** life was very hard.*

7 We use ***whose*** to refer to something owned by someone:
*Mr Gordon, **whose** house was for sale, invited us in.*

2 Susan is showing her photographs to a friend. Use the prompts to make sentences for her. The first one is done for you.

a Catherine (I met her on holiday last year.)
This is Catherine, who I met on holiday last year.

b Keith's guitar (once played by Eric Clapton)
Keith bought this ....

c Robert (getting married next week)
That's ....

d We had lunch in town in the new restaurant. (opened by David Beckham)
We had ....

e My friend Mark (I often play tennis with him.)
That's ....

f Laurie (She's going to live in Australia.)
This girl is ....

g We had a lovely time at the party. (all the family was together)
We ....

3 **Read the text and complete the exercise that follows.**

Jake Houseman decided to be a computer wizard, so he first went and asked his brother Martin for advice. Martin was out, so he asked his other brother, Paul, what to do. Paul told him about a shop called Computer Solutions, which was very cheap, so he went there and bought a 'Century' (a very new type of computer).

As he was taking the boxes from the car, his neighbour Geraldine (from the house on the left) asked him what he had bought. Then Roy, Geraldine's dog, bit him on the left leg and he dropped the printer on his foot. He went to see his doctor, Miriam Barrett, and she told him to go to hospital. When he got there, another doctor, Jacky Sewell, told him he had nothing to worry about and sent him home. When he got home, his other neighbour Gloria (from the house on the right) asked him if she could use his new computer. He agreed, but Gloria's dog Rex bit his other leg and once again he had to go back to hospital. This time a third doctor, Jordan Freeman, gave him a bed and he spent the night there.

When he got home he decided that he wanted to live in a penthouse flat, or anywhere where there were no dogs!

Write sentences about the people, places and animals from the text, using *who*, *which*, *that* or *whose*. The first one is done for you.

a Martin, who is Jake's brother, was out when he called on him.

b Paul, ..., gave him some advice.

c He went to Computer Solutions, ..., and bought a computer.

d He bought a 'Century', ..., and took it home.

e Geraldine, ..., asked him what he had bought.

f Roy, ..., bit him on the left leg.

g Miriam Barrett, ..., told him to go to the hospital.

h Jacky Sewell, ..., sent him home.

i Gloria, ..., asked if she could use his computer.

j Rex, ..., bit him on the right leg.

k Jordan Freeman, ..., gave him a bed in the hospital.

l A penthouse flat, ..., is a place where there are no dogs.

C Mixed practice

defining and non-defining relative clauses

1 Complete the following sentences with an appropriate relative pronoun from the box. Where more than one pronoun is possible, write both. The first one is done for you.

that
where
which
who
whose

a I bought a computer ...that/which... I saw in a magazine.
b I don't like people .... talk about computers all the time.
c Mary Clark, ... my brother is engaged to, is a computer programmer.
d I have a mobile phone .... is smaller than a watch.
e She's a computer criminal .... virus caused millions of dollars of damage to big companies.
f My friend Jeff, ... wallet was stolen, has cancelled all his credit cards.
g You can buy contact lenses .... change the colour of your eyes.
h Tansi is the name of my mother's dog .... died last spring.
i Andy, ... won first prize in the programming competition, has got a job at Computer Solutions.
j The library is the room .... people can read in peace.

2 Complete the sentences with an appropriate relative pronoun. Do not use one if it is not necessary.

a The other day I bumped into a woman .... I used to go to school with.
b I will never forget some of the people .... went to that school.
c She suggested going to a restaurant .... she knew.
d We sat at a table .... was in a dark corner.
e The waiter .... served us seemed very friendly.
f My friend, ... was sitting opposite me, started talking in a whisper.
g She told me about some criminals .... she knew.
h She said they were people .... used computers to rob banks.
i I couldn't believe the information .... she gave me.
j I took out my mobile phone, ... I had in my handbag, and made a phone call.
k The person I called was a friend .... had recently been promoted to sergeant in the police force.
l On the way out of the restaurant I was stopped by a man .... expression was not friendly. It was the nice waiter.
m 'You're not the kind of person .... we want in this restaurant', he growled.
n I looked for the friend .... had brought me here. But she had gone.

3 Combine the following pairs of sentences using a relative pronoun. The beginning of each sentence is given. The first one is done for you.

a (Some drivers drive too slowly … Some drivers are really annoying.)

Drivers who drive too slowly are really annoying.

b (He wanted to wear the jacket … His wife had given him the jacket.)

He wanted ....

c (I can still remember the day … You got back from university on that day.)

I can..........

d (I don't like people … Some people smoke all the time.)

I don't ....

e (I like this kind of soup …. It is hot and freshly made.)

The kind of..........

f (Last week I met someone … I hadn't seen him for months.)

Last week ....

g (My friend Steve likes that kind of music … I just can't bear that kind.)

The kind ....

h (She will never forget the moment …They announced the winner.)

She ....

i (I was reading a book when you saw me … It was very interesting.)

The book..........

j (That's the director of *The Multitude* … His latest film made a million dollars.)

That's ....

UNIT 11

A The past of modals (1)

possibility, ability and certainty

1 Read this explanation of the past forms of modal verbs. (For a definition of modal verbs, see Unit 8.)

possibility

1 We use ***may have***, ***might have*** or ***could have*** + *past participle* to say something possibly happened in the past:

Frances ***may have left*** *her purse on the bus.*
She ***might have left*** *it in the cinema.*
Someone ***could have found*** *the purse and picked it up.*

2 When we want to say that something possibly did not happen, we use ***might not have*** or ***may not have***:

Denise ***might not have caught*** *the plane.*
She ***may not have got*** *to the airport in time.*

3 We use ***could have*** to say that something was possible but we did not do it:

I ***could have bought*** *a return train ticket but I decided to just get a single.*

ability and permission

4 We can use ***could*** + *infinitive* for ability at any time in the past:

My grandfather ***could write*** *shorthand in Spanish.*

But we usually use ***was able to*** or ***managed to*** particularly when we are talking about a specific event:

Diana ***was able to open*** *the heavy door.* NOT: ~~*Diana could open the heavy door*~~.
She ***managed to get*** *out.* NOT: ~~*She could get out*~~.

5 We can use ***couldn't*** + *infinitive* to talk about specific or general past inability:

The receptionist ***couldn't find*** *the key.*

6 When we want to say that something was allowed at any time in the past, we can use ***could*** + *infinitive*:

I ***could play*** *the organ in the church whenever I wanted to.*

But to talk about permission at a specific time we use ***was allowed to***:

I ***was allowed to fly*** *the plane for a few minutes.*

7 We can use ***couldn't*** to talk about what was not allowed:

We ***couldn't go*** *through the main entrance. The guard told us to go to the back entrance.*

certainty

8 We use ***must have*** + *past participle* when we want to say we are certain of something in the past:

You ***must have been*** *very hot in Egypt this summer.*

9 When we think something definitely did not happen we use ***can't have*** or ***couldn't have*** + *past participle*:

Jack ***can't have seen*** *Paul on the train. Paul was in Spain last week.*
You ***can't have failed*** *your exam! You worked so hard.*
Paula ***couldn't have been*** *late today. She left really early.*

2 Read the following sentences and underline the past modals; then write the number of the explanation above that refers to each. The first one is done for you.

PAULINE: You were really late this morning. Sergeant Humphreys must have been furious! (a explanation 8)

JANET: He was! I could have taken the bus, (b ....) but it was raining so hard I ran to the underground, but I couldn't get a train because there was a strike. (c ....)

PAULINE: It's a pity you didn't come by car.

JANET: Yes, I wish I had taken my car, then I could have got here on time. (d ....)

PAULINE: But you might have got stuck in the traffic anyway. (e ....) Would you like some coffee? You can't have had time for one yet. (f ....)

JANET: I'd love one! Sergeant Humphreys said I couldn't have one when I got in. (g ....) I was really annoyed!

PAULINE: Oh well. He may have forgiven you! (h ....)

JANET: But I might not have forgiven him! (i ....)

3 Some people copy the work of famous writers (like Shakespeare) or artists (like Picasso). For each sentence in the left-hand column write the number of the sentence from the right-hand column that best explains it. The first one is done for you.

a Shakespeare can't have written that play. It's not his style. [7]
b Someone might have used his name. [ ]
c Shakespeare must have been a very good playwright. [ ]
d Picasso couldn't have painted this picture. It's too boring. [ ]
e Paula King, the famous woman forger, could have copied Picasso's style. [ ]
f I don't think anyone but Picasso could have painted it! [ ]
g Shakespeare might have written this play. The words sound like his. [ ]
h Picasso sold a lot of paintings during his life. He must have been very rich. [ ]

1 I am sure that he wasn't poor.
2 It is certain that he was.
3 It is impossible that anyone else did it.
4 It is not possible that he painted it.
5 It is possible that someone did.
6 It's possible that he did.
7 It's not possible that he did it.
8 It's possible that she did.

4 Rewrite the sentences using an appropriate modal verb. Sometimes more than one answer is possible. The first one is done for you.

a It is possible that Picasso painted this picture, but I can't be sure.
Picasso could/might have painted this picture

b He painted the whole picture in two hours? That's just not possible. ....

c Look at all those paintings in her private gallery. I'm sure she was rich. ....

d The thieves possibly took the painting during the night.
....

B The past of modals (2)

obligation and advisability

1

obligation

1 To talk about obligation in the past we use ***had to*** + *infinitive*:
Mrs Grant ***had to change*** *the shoes because they were too small.*
Note: We do not use ***have got to*** in the past tense – we use ***had to***.

2 To say someone was not obliged to do something we use ***didn't have to***:
I ***didn't have to pay*** *for the second cup of coffee.*

advisability

3 When we want to say something was advisable but did not happen we use ***should have*** or ***ought to have*** + *past participle*:
You really ***should have telephoned*** *me.*
I ***ought to have had*** *the news first.*
Note: We don't use ***had better*** to talk about the past – we use ***should have*** or ***ought to have***.

4 When we want to say that something happened that we did not want, we use ***shouldn't have*** + *past participle*:
The Smith's ***shouldn't have left*** *so early. They missed the dessert.*

5 When we want to say something was or was not necessary we use ***needed to*** or ***didn't need to*** + *infinitive*:
Robin ***didn't need to see*** *the manager today.* (It wasn't necessary.)
He ***needed to see*** *Mr Collins instead.* (It was necessary.)

2 Read the following sentences and underline the modal verb, then write which of the above explanations (1–5) applies to each one.

a When I worked for the government I had to start work at 8.30.
explanation 1

b I didn't need to take a bus as I lived round the corner.
....

c I should have stayed there longer as I would have got a pay rise.
....

d I didn't have to wear a uniform. ....

e My friend Leonard had to destroy the old files. ....

f He had to sign a document promising not to read them.
....

g He shouldn't have even looked at them. ....

h No, but they didn't have to fire him! ....

3 Read the article about the Roman army in Britain 2,000 years ago. Choose the correct phrase in the box to complete each gap. Some of them are used more than once. The first one is done for you.

didn't have to
had to
needed to
should have
shouldn't have
didn't need to

Roman soldiers (**a**) ......had to...... be very disciplined. They (**b**) .... think about anything but fighting. Everything they did was just what they (**c**) .... do. They (**d**) .... worry about food, as the Roman generals believed that feeding the soldiers well was very important. However, the officers (**e**) .... given them better clothing, as the soldiers in England were very unhappy because they did not have warm clothing. Because the climate was so bad they (**f**) .... write home to their mothers to send them socks and underwear. They tried to conquer the whole British Isles, and they (**g**) .... fight very hard to take England. However, they (**h**) .... fought against the Scots, because they were extremely fierce fighters! In 122 CE (almost 1,900 years ago) when Hadrian was Caesar, they (**i**) .... start building a huge wall right across the country to keep the Scots out. Then they (**j**) .... patrol the wall constantly. They (**k**) .... given up, as it cost them a lot of money to keep the garrison. The Scots (**l**) .... spend anything as they had very simple weapons and ate local food, and they (**m**) .... send home to Italy for socks! The wall (**n**) .... be abandoned over 1,600 years ago, in 383 CE.

C Mixed practice

The past of modals

1 Rewrite the expressions in blue, in the following sentences, using either *must have*, *couldn't have* or *might have*. The first one is done for you.

CUSTOMS OFFICIAL: I believe you thought that we wouldn't search you.

a You must have thought ....

TRAVELLER: What on earth? I'm sure somebody put them in my bag.

b ....

CUSTOMS OFFICIAL: It isn't possible that someone else put them in your bag. You said you packed your bag yourself.

c ....

TRAVELLER: Perhaps someone who works for the airline put them in my bag.

d ....

CUSTOMS OFFICIAL: It's not possible that someone who works here put the diamonds in your bag.

e ....

TRAVELLER: Well, perhaps someone put them in my bag at home and I didn't notice.

f ....

CUSTOMS OFFICIAL: Yes, and possibly it was your fairy godmother! You're under arrest!

g ....

2 Circle the correct modal verb in blue.

TEACHER: Someone took the statue of Shakespeare from this classroom. Who was it?
ANGELA: It (**a**) ought to/must have been the school cleaner, sir.
TEACHER: Why do you say that?
ANGELA: Because it (**b**) couldn't/might have been anyone from this class. We're not like that.
TEACHER: Oh come on Angela, it (**c**) might/didn't need to have been any of you. Did someone take it as a joke?
ALL THE STUDENTS: Sir!
TEACHER: Well really. It (**d**) can't/ought to have been the cleaner. I mean, why would she do such a thing?
ANGELA: OK sir, but if it wasn't the cleaner it (**e**) might/should have been Miss Williams.
TEACHER: Miss Williams? Why? You really (**f**) didn't need to/shouldn't make accusations like that!
ANGELA: Well, because she likes, ummm, sculptures.
TEACHER: Oh don't be ridiculous. It (**g**) couldn't/should have been Miss Williams. She teaches art, for heaven's sake, not literature.
ANGELA: But sir, that's why it (**h**) couldn't/must have been her. She (**i**) had to/should have it for her classes to draw Shakespeare.
SIMON: Sir?
TEACHER: What, Simon?
SIMON: It (**j**) can't/didn't need to have been Miss Williams. She was away sick yesterday and Shakespeare was taken before she …
TEACHER: Yes, Simon? Go on.
SIMON: Nothing, sir.
TEACHER: Nothing, sir? You know something about this, don't you?
SIMON: I (**k**) couldn't/might do, sir.
TEACHER: Well then, was it you? Did you steal Shakespeare?
SIMON: Oh no sir. It (**l**) couldn't/shouldn't have been me.
TEACHER: Why not?
SIMON: Because, well, Shakespeare and me, well, we don't get on! You (**m**) should/can't have known that, sir.

UNIT 12

A Conditional sentences (1) first and zero conditionals

1 Read this explanation.

conditional sentences

1 We use *conditional sentences* when we want to say that something is the consequence of or depends on something else:

the condition	the consequence
If it rains	*I will get wet.*
If I was rich	*I would buy an aeroplane.*

The ***if*** clause can come first or second in a sentence:

If there are any tickets left we can see the film tomorrow.
We can see the film tomorrow ***if*** *there are any tickets left.*

2 We sometimes use an *imperative verb* in the second clause when the ***if*** clause refers to the present or future:

If you're going to play your guitar, ***do*** *it quietly!*
If you send him a card, ***put*** *my name on it too.*

first condtional

3 We use the *first conditional* when we are talking about something that may happen in the future. In this type of conditional sentence, we usually choose ***will*** for the consequence clause, with the ***if*** clause in the *present simple*:

If I ***lose*** *my job I* ***will*** *emigrate.*
She'll marry him if he asks her.

Note: we can use the continuous form in a conditional sentence:

If you tell him the truth you ***will be doing*** *the right thing.*

4 We can use other modal verbs such as ***can*** and ***may***, and even ***be going to*** in place of ***will***:

If Julia comes this evening, we ***can*** *go to the cinema.*
We ***may*** *go to see Terminator 3 if it's not sold out.*
As soon as Jack finishes the book ***I'm going to*** *read it.*

zero conditional

5 We use the *zero conditional* when we are talking about things that are generally true all the time. In this type of conditional we use the *present simple* in both clauses:

If you ***heat*** *wax it (always)* ***melts.***
The dog ***runs*** *away if we* ***leave*** *the door open.*

Note: we can use the continuous form in a zero conditional:

When I ***am running*** *I always get out of breath.*

2 Write what the man is saying, using the clauses in the boxes. Start each sentence with the second clause from the sentence before. The first one is done for you.

a go to the shop
b buy a lottery ticket
c watch the lottery programme on TV this evening
d probably be disappointed

a If I need some more milk
I'll go to the shop.
b If I go to the shop, ...
c ....
d ....

e buy a boat
f sail to the USA.
g visit Las Vegas.
h lose all my money.

e If I win the lottery ....
f ....
g ....
h ....

3 Match up the two halves of the sentences in the boxes.

a If I finish my work before 5
b Barbara won't be able to go swimming
c If it snows
d Tom won't be happy
e If Jenny loses her glasses
f If the taxi arrives soon
g If Jonathan wants to close a file on his computer

1 she'll be very upset.
2 he always saves it first.
3 if they don't buy him a cat for his birthday.
4 I'll give you a lift home.
5 Mr and Mrs Thompson will be able to get to the airport in time for their flight.
6 if she forgets her costume.
7 we'll need to put chains on the car wheels.

a ....
b ....
c ....
d ....
e ....
f ....
g ....

B Conditional sentences (2) second and third conditionals

1 **Read this explanation.**

second conditional

1 We use the *second conditional* to talk about the consequence of impossible or unlikely events or situations in the present or future. The verb pattern is past simple in the ***if*** clause and ***would*** + *infinitive* in the consequence clause:

the condition	the consequence
*If there **was** a war*	*the stock market **would boom**.*
*If I **passed** Meg on the street*	*I **wouldn't recognise** her.*

2 We often use the *subjunctive* form ***were*** in place of ***was*** in the ***if*** clause, especially in phrases giving advice:

*If I **were** you I wouldn't spend so much on clothes.*
*I would punish that dog if it **were** mine.*

3 We often abbreviate the ***would*** after a pronoun:

*We**'d** send him a card if we knew the address.*
*I don't know if he**'d** reply.*

4 We use ***even if*** to mean **'it wouldn't matter if'** and ***unless*** to mean **'if … not'**:

***Even if** he was the king she wouldn't marry him.* (= It wouldn't matter if he was the king, she still wouldn't marry him.)
*I wouldn't vote for her **unless** she changed her policies.* (= … if she did not change her policies.)

5 We often use the conditional ***would*** form without an ***if*** *clause* when we want to ask questions or make requests in a polite way:

***Would** you **pass** me the milk, please?*
***I'd like to give** you a small gift.*

third conditional

6 The *third conditional* is used to express the imagined consequences of something that didn't happen in the past:

If I'd caught the bus (but I didn't catch the bus) *I would have arrived at work on time.* (The consequence of catching the bus – but I can only imagine it because it didn't happen!)

7 We use the *past perfect* in the ***if*** clause, and ***would have*** + *past participle* in the consequence clause:

*If Carol **had given** me her purse to look after she **wouldn't have lost** it.*
*Phoebe **would have played** in the hockey team if she **had brought** her kit.*

8 We can use the continuous form of the verb in either or both clauses:

*If David **had been watching** the match he **would have seen** that amazing goal!*
*Jane **would have been working** today if she **hadn't been visiting** her mother.*

2 Complete the dialogue with one word in each gap.

MAN: Taxi! Taxi!
DRIVER: Where (**a**) .... you like to go, sir?
MAN: Harrington Square, please.
DRIVER: Right you are, sir. There's a lot of traffic today. Do you think it (**b**) .... be quicker if I went through Austin Street?
MAN: Not sure about that. If I (**c**) .... you, I think I'd go round by the park.
DRIVER: Too late for that now, sir, though I would (**d**) .... done that yesterday – but this morning I got stuck for hours on the roundabout.
MAN: OK, I take your point. It's my fault, anyway. If I had left a bit earlier I would (**e**) .... missed the rush hour altogether.
DRIVER: You're not to blame, sir. If this taxi only went a bit faster we (**f**) ....be halfway there ...
MAN: Watch out!
DRIVER: Phew! That was close!
MAN: Yes, it certainly was. If you (**g**) .... braked so quickly you (**h**) .... have hit that cyclist and probably killed him! How about driving just a bit more slowly?
DRIVER: Sorry, sir. But if cyclists (**i**) .... take so many risks they wouldn't have so many accidents. Anyway, I'd better hurry – otherwise you won't get to Harrington Square on time.
MAN: Actually, I think I (**j**) .... prefer to be late!
DRIVER: That's your decision, sir, but if you (**k**) .... not worried about the time ...
MAN: Yes, what?
DRIVER: Well, I mean why did you ask me to get there as fast as possible?
MAN: I didn't.
DRIVER: Didn't you?

3 Rewrite the sentences using *if* or *if ... not* and the second or third conditional. Use the phrases in blue (but you may have to change the form of the verb and change affirmative statements into negative ones).

a Change my job? I'm not going to, of course. But I like the idea of being a teacher.

If I changed my job I would be a teacher.

b I wasn't listening to the radio. That's the reason why I didn't hear about the traffic jams on the motorway.

....

c I'm a gardener. I spend all my time outdoors. Nice idea, but it's not going to happen! It's just my imagination.

....

d My dream is to win the lottery and buy a new house – but it's not going to happen.

....

C Mixed practice

zero, first, second and third conditions

1 **Read the sentences and then write the correct form of the verb in brackets. The first one is done for you.**

a If you ......were...... (be) my sister, I ..would give.. (give) you my honest opinion but you aren't, so I won't!

b I .... (be) completely amazed if you .... (come) last in the race. But it's not going to happen so I don't need to worry, do I?

c If I .... (be) you, I .... (not/say) that again. That's my advice anyway.

d Before you speak I must just tell you that if you .... (say) that again, I .... (get) really cross. So don't do it, OK?

e It's going to be a tough race, but I have confidence in you. If you .... (win), I .... (be) really happy.

f The light's going. Why are we waiting? If the race .... (not/start) soon it .... (be) dark.

g We're brothers, but even if you .... (be/not) my brother I .... (still/be) on your side.

h You need a rest. If I .... (be) you, I .... (stop) training for a week.

2 **Circle the correct answer to the questions about the following pairs of sentences.**

a 1 *I wouldn't go to see that band even if you bought me a ticket.*
2 *I wouldn't have been to see that band if you hadn't bought me a ticket.*
Which sentence means you went to see the band? 1 or 2? ....

b 1 *If I had gone on that television quiz show, I would have won a million pounds.*
2 *If I go on that television quiz show, I'll win a million pounds.*
Which sentence means that you think you're going to go on the TV show? 1 or 2? ....

c 1 *If she plays well, she'll get a place on the team.*
2 *If she played well, she'd get a place on the team.*
Which sentence suggests that she is more likely to get a place on the team? 1 or 2? ....

d 1 *The teacher would have forgotten the homework if Vita hadn't reminded her.*
2 *If Vita doesn't remind the teacher, she forgets the homework.*
Which sentence means that the teacher didn't forget the homework? 1 or 2? ....

e 1 *If you train properly, you get fit.*
2 *If you trained properly, you'd get fit.*
Which sentence refers to everybody? 1 or 2? ....

f 1 *If I were young, I would take up squash.*
2 *I wouldn't have taken up squash if I didn't feel young.*
Which sentence means you have taken up squash? 1 or 2? ....

g 1 *If they play like this, they'll win in the final.*
2 *If they had played like this, they would have won in the final.*
Which sentence means that the final has already happened? 1 or 2? ....

3 Read this text.

They invited Kevin Harley to the annual international sales conference in Amsterdam. When Kevin Harley is around, disaster strikes! He had a front-row seat. Anthea Donnelly was invited to open the meeting. She stood up to walk over to the projector. Kevin had his feet stuck out in front of him. She tripped over his feet and fell on to the projector. The projector fell over and all the slides were mixed up on the floor. The wire came out of the projector and the lights were fused. It went dark. Everyone began to panic and scramble over the seats to get out. Kevin lit a match and the fire sprinklers came on. It was chaos.

Next year I don't think they will invite him!

Using the information in the text, put the words in the box in the gaps in these sentences. You may have to change the form of the verbs.

be	want
fall	fuse
have	wouldn't
if	light
will	have not
have	

a If Kevin had not been invited, everything would have .... all right.

b He wouldn't have caused any trouble if he had not .... a front-row seat.

c .... Anthea Donnelly had not been invited to open the meeting, she wouldn't have fallen over him.

d It would have been better if she hadn't .... to use the projector.

e If Kevin had not stuck his feet out, she ....have tripped over him.

f If the projector had not .... over, the wire wouldn't have come out of it.

g The lights wouldn't have gone out if the wire .... come out of the projector.

h If the lights hadn't ...., the people wouldn't have panicked.

i Kevin wouldn't have .... a match if it hadn't gone dark suddenly.

j If the fire alarm .... been less sensitive, the match wouldn't have started the sprinklers.

k If they invite him next year I think they .... make him sit at the back!

A Verb patterns (1)

verb + *ing* form and verb + *to* + infinitive

1 Read this explanation.

verb + *-ing* form

1 When we want to use two *verbs* together we often use the *-ing* form of the second verb:

*I really **enjoy swimming** in the sea.*
*Kate **imagined competing** in the final.*

Some verbs are always followed by the *-ing* form. These are verbs such as:
admit, avoid, consider, deny, dislike, enjoy, finish, imagine, involve, miss, risk, suggest
and *phrasal* verbs such as:
carry on, give up, keep on, put off

verb + *to* + infinitive

2 After certain verbs we always use ***to*** + *infinitive*:

*George **decided to buy** a new car.*
*Grace didn't **dare to tell** her boss the truth.*

Other verbs of this type are:
agree, appear, arrange, attempt, dare, decide, fail, forget, hope, learn, manage, offer, plan, pretend, promise, refuse, seem, tend, threaten, want

2 Which is the correct sentence in each pair? Circle 1 or 2.

a 1 Isla enjoys to listen to jazz.
  2 Isla enjoys listening to jazz.

b 1 She offered to buy her friend a ticket to a jazz concert.
  2 She offered buying her friend a ticket to a jazz concert.

c 1 He agreed to go with her.
  2 He agreed going with her.

d 1 She suggested to meet at seven o'clock.
  2 She suggested meeting at seven o'clock.

e 1 He promised arriving on time.
  2 He promised to arrive on time.

f 1 Isla expected to see him outside the jazz club.
  2 Isla expected seeing him outside the jazz club.

g 1 The next day he denied forgetting about their arrangement!
  2 The next day he denied to forget about their arrangement!

3 **Circle the correct alternative, in blue, in the following sentences. The first one is done for you**

a My brother wanted to go/going to the cinema with me.

b He suggested to go/going later that evening and I agreed.

c In the afternoon I decided to go/going and see my friend.

d I promised to get/getting home in time.

e I enjoyed to see/seeing my friend.

f We decided to play/playing tennis.

g We both managed to win/winning some games.

h We finished to play/playing quite late, just as it was getting dark.

i On the way home I avoided going/to go on the motorway.

j I forgot turning/to turn right at the traffic lights and I got completely lost.

k When the police stopped me I denied to go/going too fast.

l I admitted being/to be lost.

m I dislike to be/being lost.

n In the end the police agreed letting/to let me go.

o I got home far too late, but I offered to go/going to the cinema with my brother on a different evening.

4 **When the actor Tony Forbes reached his 60th birthday, his friends gave him a party. Read the speech he made at the party and write the correct form of the verbs. The first one is done for you**

What a fantastic party for my 60th birthday. I (**a**) appear to have (appear/have) a lot of friends. That makes me very happy.

When I was a young man my father (**b**) .... (agree/let) me study acting and he (**c**) .... (offer/pay) for it, but I said no because I (**d**) .... (want/do) it on my own. I had great dreams, you know. I (**e**) .... (imagine/star) in films, but I (**f**) (fail/become) .... a really big star. Still, life is not so bad. I've (**g**) .... (enjoy/do) small parts in films, although I (**h**) .... (admit/be) disappointed sometimes when I haven't (**i**) .... (manage/get) the lead role.

When I've finished this film I (**j**) .... (plan/stop) acting. I (**k**) .... (hope/go) and live abroad. I (**l**) .... (want/be) somewhere where there is sun, you see. Of course, I'll (**m**) .... (miss/work) with all the other actors, but I've (**n**) .... (promise/keep) in touch with my friends.

I (**o**) .... (dislike/say) goodbye. I (**p**) .... (tend/prefer) 'see you later'. And that's what I hope. That I will see you all later. Thank you all for this lovely party. I will never forget it.

B Verb patterns (2)

verb + *ing* form or + *to* + infinitive, verb + *that* clause

1 Read this explanation.

verb + *-ing*, or + *to* + infinitive

1 Some *verbs* can be followed by either the ***-ing*** form or ***to*** + *infinitive* without any change to the meaning. These are verbs such as:

love, hate, begin, start, continue, intend, not bother

*Tom **loves to go** for long walks in the country.* (= Tom loves going for long walks in the country.)

*Pete **began to study** French.* (= Pete began studying French.)

2 Other verbs can be followed by either the ***-ing*** form or ***to*** + *infinitive* but the meaning is different. Compare the different meanings with these verbs.

never forget:

*I'll **never forget seeing** the Eiffel Tower for the first time.* (= Seeing the Eiffel Tower for the first time was fantastic. I'll never forget it.)

*I'll **never forget to see** if there is enough petrol in the fuel tank again.* (= I must see if there is enough petrol in the tank in the future. I'm not going to forget it.)

Note: ***never forget*** behaves differently from ***forget*** on its own.

remember:

*David **remembered meeting** Sally.* (= David remembered that he had met Sally.)

*David **remembered to meet** Sally.* (= He had arranged to meet her, he remembered the arrangement and did it.)

stop:

*I think you should **stop painting the wall**.* (= I think you should not paint any more.)

*I think you should **stop to paint the wall**.* (= I think you should stop what you are doing and paint the wall.)

try:

*I **tried to open** the window but it was stuck.* (= I couldn't open it.)

*I **tried opening** the window but it was still too hot.* (= I opened the window but it did not make the room cooler.)

3 We can use both the ***-ing*** form and ***to*** + *infinitive* after the verb ***like***, but the meaning is slightly different. We usually use the ***-ing*** form when we want to say that we enjoy something:

*Sue **likes relaxing** at home.* (= Sue enjoys relaxing at home.)

And we use the ***to*** + *infinitive* form when we want to say that we usually choose to do something:

*I **like to wear** a hat in the sun.* (= I prefer to wear a hat in the sun.)

After ***not like*** we can use the ***-ing*** *form* or ***to*** + *infinitive* with no difference in meaning.

4 After ***would like*** we use the ***to*** + *infinitive* form:

***Would** you **like to come** round on Sunday?*

***Would** Andy **like to have** another sandwich?*

verb + *that* + clause

5 These verbs can also be followed by ***that*** + clause:

admit, agree, decide, deny, expect, forget, promise, remember, suggest

*They **agreed** to leave.* → *They **agreed that** they should leave.*

*Helen **forgot** to pay the fine.* → *Helen **forgot that** she had to pay the fine.*

*Jane **promised** to phone.* → *Jane **promised that** she would phone.*

*Paul **suggested** phoning the police.* → *Paul **suggested that** we should phone the police.*

2 **What exactly do the following sentences mean? The first one is done for you.**

a She stopped to tie her shoelaces. She stopped what she was doing and tied her shoelaces.

b She remembered meeting him at a concert. ....

c Keith forgot sending that letter to his friend. ....

d I stopped running and had a rest. ....

e I hope you remember to phone me. ....

f Julie forgot to water the plants. ....

g We never stop talking, you and I! ....

3 **Write the correct word or words in the gaps, using the words in the brackets. Sometimes more than one answer is possible. The first one is done for you.**

When the policeman arrested Ruth in the supermarket and took her to the police station, she admitted (a) that she had (she/have) some things in her bag she had not paid for, but she denied (b) .... (she/take) them. She began (c) .... (offer) to pay for the things straight away so that she could take her six-year-old daughter Jane home, but the policeman told her to stop (d) .... (talk), and said that he intended (e) .... (take) action over the incident.

At that moment, Jane started (f) .... (cry). When the police officer asked what the matter was, Ruth said that her daughter hated (g) .... (listen) to their conversation. The officer said that he did not like (h) .... (be) unkind, but he could not ignore a crime like this. But he agreed to stop (i) .... (ask) questions until Jane was happier.

When Jane finally stopped (j) .... (cry), She told them that she had put the things in her mother's bag. Jane didn't realise that her mother would get into trouble. In the end the police officer decided (k) .... (he/believe) Jane. He agreed (l) .... (he/be) a bit unkind, but he suggested (m) .... (Ruth/watch) her daughter a bit more carefully. Ruth promised (n) .... (she/do) that and left the police station a sadder but wiser person.

C Mixed practice

verb patterns

1 **Rewrite the sentences using the *to + infinitive* or *-ing* form of the verb in brackets. The first one is done for you.**

a I play tennis. (enjoy)

I enjoy playing tennis.

b I'll finish the job in a couple of hours. (expect)

....

c Phil: 'I didn't borrow her bicycle.' (deny)

....

d Phil: 'I'll mend it.' (offer)

....

e Phil: 'I'll buy a new bell.' (agree)

....

f I didn't do any work yesterday. (avoid)

....

g I played tennis with my cousin when I was young. (remember)

....

h I am going to Italy this summer. (want)

....

i Phil: 'Buy a new computer.' (suggest)

....

j Me: 'I'll do it.' (decide)

....

k My cousin didn't come to play tennis with me. (forget)

....

2 **Complete the following sentences using a form of the verb *skydive*, either *to skydive* or *skydiving*. The first one is done for you.**

a I asked my mother for advice on a new hobby and she suggested skydiving .

b My best friend loves ....

c When the police questioned Gary he denied ....

d He said he wouldn't dare ....

e I can't! I've never learnt ....

f Karen hates ....

g When they met she was pretending ....

h Michael suddenly realised that he had always hoped ....

i After the accident, they stopped .... forever.

3 **Make sentences by matching words from columns A and B. Each phrase can only be used once. The first one is done for you**

Column A	Column B
a Jack admitted	1 playing football by pretending he was ill.
b He denied	2 being in Bob's room.
c Jack managed to avoid	3 to go home yet.
d I didn't see you yesterday. At least I don't remember	4 playing the cello when I left school.
e I don't like sport and I hate	5 seeing you.
f I know I've lied in the past but this time I promise	6 taking Bob's money.
g Would you like	7 to tell you the truth.
h I still like singing but I stopped	8 to take his drumsticks to the rehearsal.
i I know it's late but I don't want	9 to share my pizza?
j My shoe felt loose so I stopped	10 watching it.
k The drummer forgot	11 to tie my shoelace.

a ....2.... e .... i ....

b .... f .... j ....

c .... g .... k ....

d .... h ....

4 **Rewrite the following sentences inserting *that* where it should go. The first one is done for you.**

a Mary agreed to go skating.

Mary agreed that she would go skating.

b Ann forgot to phone her boss.

....

c Tom promised to help with the house move.

....

d Jo denied eating Graham's sandwiches.

....

e Graham promised to forget about it.

....

f Sue remembered eating the cake.

....

g Arthur agreed he had behaved badly.

....

UNIT 14

A Direct and indirect speech

direct speech, indirect speech in the present and past

1 When we want to say what we or someone else has said, or thought, we can do so in two ways. We can use direct speech or indirect speech.

direct speech

1 In *direct speech* we can say exactly what was said or thought, using *verbs* like ***said***, ***thought***, ***shouted*** etc. We use inverted commas round the speech:

Paul said, 'You're late!'
I thought, 'He doesn't really like me.'

2 We can put the direct speech first (i.e. before ***said***, ***thought***, etc.). If it is first, we often put the name after the verb:

'Larry is my favourite actor,' ***said Tom.***

But if we are using a *pronoun* we always put it before the verb:

'I'm hungry!' ***he thought.***

We usually use this style in writing and not very often in speaking.

3 We sometimes use ***be like*** or ***go*** before direct speech, but only in very informal conversational English:

He's like *'are you OK?'*
She goes *'see you later.'*

Note: ***to be like*** is more common in American English.

indirect speech in the present

4 When we report what someone is saying or thinking now, we use *indirect speech* after ***says***, ***thinks***, ***hopes*** etc, with both clauses in the present tense. We often use ***that***, but it is not obligatory.

GAIL: *I'm just leaving London.* → *Gail* ***says*** *(that) she's just* ***leaving*** *London.*

We also use this form when we want to say something that is always true:

He says he ***doesn't like*** *rock music.*

When we want to report something that someone says about the *future* we use the same tense they have used in the direct speech:

KEITH: *I'***m going*** *to Boston tomorrow.* → *Keith says he'***s going*** *to Boston tomorrow.*

5 We can use verbs that express the feeling of the speaker when we report what someone has said or thought. For example, ***hope***, ***feel***, ***be afraid***, ***want***, ***wish***:

David ***hopes*** *you can get some tickets.*
He ***wants*** *to see the show tomorrow.*

indirect speech in the past

6 When we want to say what someone said to us in the past, we put the tense into the past. We change the *present simple* to the *past simple*:

KEITH: *I* ***don't have*** *time to chat.* → *Keith* ***said*** *he* ***didn't have*** *time to chat.*

When we report someone using ***will*** or ***can*** we say ***would*** or ***could***:

PAUL: *I* ***won't*** *have time!* → *He said he* ***wouldn't*** *have time.*

7 When we want to report something that was said about something that happened before the person spoke we have to use the past perfect in the indirect speech clause:

MARY: *I've just got back from New York.* → *Mary* ***said*** *she* ***had*** *just* ***got*** *back from New York.*

JOHN: *I lost my wallet in the street.* → *John* ***said*** *he* ***had lost*** *his wallet in the street.*

8 In informal speech we sometimes use the same tense that the person used in the direct speech, when we are talking about something that is still true at the moment of speaking:

HARRY: *I've got three tickets for the concert.* → *Harry* ***said*** *he's* ***got*** *three tickets for the concert.*

2 Rewrite the following things that people said in the past as indirect speech. The first one is done for you.

a 'I've lived here for two years.' (Mary)
Mary said she had lived there for two years.

b 'I study music.' (Peter) ....

c 'We work in a software company.' (Paul and Kenny) ....

d 'I will finish my course in six months.' (Mrs Yamanachi) ....

e 'I will graduate next year.' (Ellen) ....

f 'I'm going to join a rock band.' (Matt) ....

g 'My brother's going to work in a law firm in London.' (Sally) ....

h 'We've just watched a football match on TV.' (Kate and Jane) ....

i 'I've just been to New York for the first time.' (Simon) ....

j 'I'm going to marry George' (Anita) ....

k 'I'll be there in a minute!' (Henry) ....

3 Write the most appropriate form of the verb in brackets.

a He said that they .... (meet) on holiday last year.

b He said that they .... (fall) in love almost at once.

c He said that he .... (never/be) in love before.

d She said that she .... (have to) go home in two days.

e She said that she .... (can/not) stay for another week.

f She said that she .... (will) see him in three weeks.

g He said that he .... (have/not) seen her since that day.

h He said that he still .... (miss) her.

What were the speaker's actual words in each case? The first one is done for you.

i 'We met on holiday last year.'

j ....

k ....

l ....

m ....

n ....

o ....

p ....

B Other indirect speech forms

asking, wondering and telling in indirect speech

1 Read this explanation.

Indirect questions and other uses

1 When we report questions said in the past, we can use the verbs ***asked/wondered + if/whether***. We put the tense into the past:

'Can I come to the meeting?' → *He asked (me)* ***if he could*** *come to the meeting.*

'Is he a union member?' → *She wondered* ***whether he was*** *a union member.*

Notice that we change the order of the subject and the verb when we report questions:

CARLOS: *'Who was the murderer?'* → *Carlos asked me* ***who the murderer was.*** (NOT: ~~*who was the murderer*~~.)

'Where has the money gone?' → *I wondered* ***where the money had gone.*** (NOT: ~~*where had the money gone*~~.)

2 When we want to report a question at the same moment that it was said, we use the form ***want to know + if*** or *question word*. We use the same tense as that in the question:

Paul ***wants to know if*** *you have finished the washing up.*

Maria ***wants to know when*** *the train leaves.*

3 When someone asks someone to do something and we want to report it, we use ***ask/tell + someone + to + infinitive***:

The teacher ***asked Karen to stand up.***

The teacher ***told Karen to stand up.***

4 Other verbs like ***invite***, ***advise***, ***order*** and ***persuade*** behave in the same way as ***ask*** and ***tell***:

Madeleine ***invited us to come*** *to her party on Sunday.*

The teacher ***advised the class to be*** *careful with their punctuation.*

The policeman ***ordered Frank to move*** *his car.*

I ***persuaded her to leave*** *work early.*

5 When we want to say that someone told someone not to do something, we usually say ***not to*** (NOT: ~~*to not*~~):

GERALDINE: *Don't shout, Dennis!* → *She told Dennis* ***not to shout.***

MICHAEL: *Don't make such a mess.* → *He told her* ***not to make*** *such a mess.*

2 Choose the right word or words from the box to go in each gap.

had	couldn't
would be	that
taken it out	him
told	be able to
agreed	what
was	advised

Jake went to the library with me yesterday afternoon. He said he (**a**) .... a library book he wanted to return. Jenny, the librarian, asked (**b**) .... when he had borrowed it. He told her that he'd (**c**) .... five years ago. She said she was sorry but the fine (**d**) .... £122. He said he was afraid he (**e**).................... possibly pay that much. She (**f**) .... him to pay a small amount each week. He (**g**) .... to do that, but he wasn't at all happy about it. He realised (**h**) .... if he didn't pay his fine, he wouldn't (**i**) .... use the library again. He said that this would be terrible because he (**j**) .... still a student. I asked him (**k**) .... the book was. He (**l**) .... me it was a comic book about a character called Tintin.

3 Some of the following sentences have got errors in them. If the sentence is not correct underline the part of the sentence where the problem is. Write the missing words or the correct form of the words in the space under the sentence. The first one is done for you.

a Jane asked I was ready to go.

asked if I

b We wondered to be late for the film.

....

c I was talking to Mrs Grant. My sister asked me who was she.

....

d Sally wondered to go to Spain or Italy on holiday.

....

e The students thought to do the exam in the spring.

....

f I know who that man is! He's Jude Law!

....

g We are all invited to have lunch with James on Friday.

....

h I invited Mark see *Elettrica* this Friday.

....

i Why don't you tell Tom buy a newspaper while he's out?

....

4 Use the correct form of the verbs in the box to fill each gap in the following sentences. Use each verb once.

promise
invite
want
say
ask
advise
order
persuade

a Lucy .... me to come and see her new flat.

b Gordon .... he was very lucky to have got his new job.

c The officer .... the soldiers to salute the president.

d 'I'll come and visit you next week,' I.......... .

e You'll never .... him to eat meat, no matter how well you cook it! He's a vegetarian.

f I .... him to pick up the children from school today. He said he would.

g I .... him not to complain to his boss.

h I .... to know if he thinks he will win the prize. Does he think he will?

C Mixed practice

direct and indirect speech

1 Write down what Marianne (the dancer) is telling her friend about her phone call with Bob. The first one is done for you.

a MARIANNE: Are you coming round tonight?
b BOB: No, I'm going to meet my mates at the skateboard park.
c MARIANNE: Do you want to come round here later?
d BOB: No, thanks. I think it'll be too late.
e MARIANNE: Do you want to come to the ballet with me next week?
f BOB: I don't think I want to see you again.
g MARIANNE: Why? Am I too boring?
h BOB: No, of course not. It's just that I prefer girls who like skateboarding better than ballet.

a I asked Bob if he was coming round that night.
b ....
c ....
d ....
e ....
f ....
g ....
h ....

2 What does Sergeant Jones say? Report the parts of the conversation in blue, using *wants to know* and *says*. The first one is done for you.

INSPECTOR PORTWOOD: Can she see them ?
SERGEANT JONES: (a) Inspector Portwood wants to know if you can see them?
WPC GREEN: Yes, I can see them now.
SERGEANT JONES: (b) She says ....
INSPECTOR PORTWOOD: What are they doing now?
SERGEANT JONES: (c) He wants to know ....
WPC GREEN: They are sitting on a park bench.
SERGEANT JONES: (d) ....
INSPECTOR PORTWOOD: Are they talking to each other?
SERGEANT JONES: (e) ....
WPC GREEN: Yes, I think they're talking. I think they are arguing.
SERGEANT JONES: (f) ....
INSPECTOR PORTWOOD: Have they got anything in their hands?
SERGEANT JONES: (g) ....
WPC GREEN: No...yes...wait...she's passing him a small package.
SERGEANT JONES: (h) ....
INSPECTOR PORTWOOD: What's in the package?
SERGEANT JONES: (i) ....
WPC GREEN: Oh dear...it's just sandwiches. Sorry!
SERGEANT JONES: (j) ....

ANSWER KEY

UNIT 1

A 2

a lives
b gets up
c drives
d works
e wears
f is working
g is making
h leaves
i drives
j reads
k are reading
l watches
m goes
n dreams

A 3

a We know – explanation 4
b runs ... bowls ... goes – explanation 3
c are just leaving – explanation 6
d You're always telling – explanation 8
e is getting – explanation 7
f leaves ... gives ... tells – explanation 3

B 2

a Where does Marek live?
b When does he get up every morning?
c How does he get to work?
d What is he working on at the moment?
e Why is he using wood for this sculpture?
f What does he wear at work?
g Where does he have supper?
h What book are they reading?
i Who does he watch television with?
j What is he dreaming about at this moment?

B 3

a F – No, he doesn't. He gets up at about six o'clock.
b T
c F – No, he doesn't. He drives/goes to work by car.
d F – No, he doesn't. He wears old clothes and big gloves.
e T
f T
g F – No, he doesn't. He has dinner with his family.
h F – No, he isn't. He is reading Harry Potter to his children.
i F – No, they don't. They watch television.
j T

B 4

a Does Paul like jogging? Yes, he does.
b Is swimming good for you? Yes, it is.
c Is the girls' team training this afternoon? No, it isn't.
d Is the tennis tournament in July? Yes, it is.
e Do the sports coaches work in the summer? No, they don't.
f Do sportsmen and sportswomen need lots of sleep? Yes, they do.
g Is rowing a boat good exercise? Yes, it is.
h Do people need lots of protein? No, they don't.
i Is Paul changing his shoes at the moment? Yes, he is.
j Does Jenny need new trainers? Yes, she does.
k Is the gym open on Sundays? No, it isn't.
l Is Jenny running round the track now? No, she isn't.
m Does Olive want a sauna after the race? Yes, she does.
n Is the team competing in the tournament? No, it isn't.

C 1

a are
b is revising
c isn't studying
d is sitting
e reading
f are singing
g doesn't usually sit
h takes
i studies
j has
k is visiting
l is taking
m is talking
n is getting

C 2

a is
b 's attending
c works
d goes
e are discussing
f believes ... is getting
g lives ... travels
h goes
i 's staying
j 's having
k don't answer ... don't give

C 3

a Is Malcolm Clarke a member of staff there?
b When is he at work?
c What is he discussing in Warsaw?
d Does Mr Clarke believe global warming is a problem?
e Why does he believe global warming is a problem?
f Does Mr Clarke travel a lot?
g How does he travel?
h Where is he staying in Warsaw?
i Is Mr Clarke having a good time?

C 4

a lives
b takes
c doesn't drive
d doesn't enjoy
e travels
f visits
g is taking part
h is speaking
i likes
j leaves
k realises
l goes
m have
n isn't
o seems
p likes
q is growing
r making
s is feeling
t gets
u likes
v is leaving

UNIT 2

A 2

a was
b were arriving
c was raining
d was sweeping
e heard
f looked
g was standing
h speaking
i noticed
j stopped
k ran
l were you doing
m shouted
n said
o was passing
p was
q wanted

A 3

a was arriving – arrived
b was being – was
c was calling – called
d was going – went
e (correct)
f went – was going
g (correct)
h was being – was

A 4

a picture 1
b picture 3
c picture 2
d picture 3
e picture 2
f picture 3
g picture 2
h picture 4
i picture 1

B 2

a got ... saw .... had left
b wondered .. had happened
c noticed .... had made
d was ... 'd locked
e was ... had smashed
f guessed .. had broken in
g went ... saw .. had gone
h had not had ... came
i had looked ... phoned.

j told ... had taken
k said ... had done
l hadn't touched ... called
m hoped ... had not been
n had finished ... made
o was ... hadn't taken

B 3

a had made ... went
b had worked ... retired
c could not ... had forgotten
d had not eaten ... was
e had washed and changed ... called
f wanted ... had read
g arrived ... had missed

B 4

a No, she wasn't sure she'd posted a letter to him.
b No, he hadn't got a letter from her.
c Yes, she hoped that she hadn't posted a letter to him.
d No, he hadn't remembered to check the post recently.
e Yes, she'd accepted a new job in a foreign country.
f No, he hadn't heard about it.
g No, she wasn't sure that she'd made the right decision.
h Yes, he'd asked her to marry him three days ago.
i Yes, she'd agreed to marry him.

C 1

a arrived, arrived
b was/were, been
c brought, brought
d bought, bought
e did, done
f ate, eaten
g felt, felt
h got, got
i had, had
j saw, seen
k met, met
l knew, known
m rang, rung
n sent, sent
o started, started
p drank, drunk
q told, told

C 2

a What did Tim ask you then?
b Why had he come over to speak to you?
c What was he talking about?
d When did Diana get there?
e When did you first see Tim?
f What did you say?
g Why did you say that?
h What did you think about that?
i Who were you waiting for?

C 3

a Question e
b Question i
c Question d
d Question c
e Question b
f Question h
g Question a
h Question f
i Question g

C 4

a decided, didn't tell, planned, reached, looked, thought, had packed, wasn't, came, couldn't, tried, kept, was beginning, was stumbling, went, hurt, fainted, had broken, was getting, was, hadn't come, was, had happened, rang, woke up, was, was, realised, had been, heard, waved, shouted, was, didn't know, had been, had searched, were, had decided, saw, was, had crawled, was shouting
b 29
c 4
d 9

UNIT 3

A 2

a Most
b A lot of/Many
c A lot of/Many
d Few/Not many
e many
f Many/A lot of
g Some
h every

A 3

a a few/some
b any
c Lots of/A lot of
d some/a few
e lots of/a lot of
f lot of
g many
h some/a few
i All
j Most
k no

B 2

a much
b all
c no
d most
e some/a bit of
f a lot of

B 3

a much
b a little
c lots
d much
e some
f any
g all
h few
i a bit
j lots of
k a bit
l no
m any

C 1

Example answers

a A lot of boys like football, but not all of them do. A few of them aren't interested at all.
b Most girls are interested in fashion, but some girls are not interested at all.
c Most young people like discos, but some prefer sports.
d I think most young people like school, but of course there are some who don't. Many children like school until they are teenagers.
e I don't think people think plays are less interesting than films. Not many people can go to the theatre so most people never go. There aren't very many theatres outside the big cities.
f A lot of old people watch television in the evening in Europe and America. But many old people have very active lives.

C 2

a ☺
b ☺
c ☹
d ☹
e ☹
f ☺
g ☹
h ☺
i ☺
j ☹

C 3

a We don't get many shoppers here any more.
b People spend very little money in this shop.
c This will only take a little time.
d There isn't any sugar in this tin.
e Everybody likes coffee.
f I always drink coffee after every meal.
g I only take a little milk in my coffee.
h I'll come round in a few minutes
i Finding a good bargain in the shops gives me a lot of satisfaction.

C 4

Example answers

a A few people eat boiled eggs.
b A few people drink water/milk.
c A lot of people eat cereal.
d Most people eat cereal.
e Some people drink fruit juice.
f Not many people eat no breakfast/boiled eggs/cooked breakfasts.
g Most people drink tea.

UNIT 4

A 2

a rule 6
b rule 2
c rule 5
d rule 1
e rule 1
f rule 3
g rule 5
h rule 2
i rule 6

A 3

Example answers

a The Regent is more expensive than the Hotel Mario. The Majestic is probably the most expensive.
b The Hotel Mario seems less comfortable than the Regent. The Majestic is the most comfortable.
c The Hotel Mario is the noisiest. The Regent is noisier than the Majestic.
d The Regent is the most modern. The Majestic is less modern than the Hotel Mario.
e The Hotel Mario seems the most crowded. The Regent seems more crowded than the Majestic.

f The Regent looks cheaper than the Majestic. The Hotel Mario looks the cheapest.
g The Hotel Mario is less luxurious than the Regent. The Majestic is the most luxurious.
h The Hotel Mario looks less peaceful than the Regent. The Majestic looks the most peaceful of all.
i I think the Hotel Regent looks more attractive than the Mario. The Majestic, of course, looks the most attractive.

B 2
a The hotter the better.
b Linda is the oldest/eldest sister.
c It's getting less and less crowded.
d It's getting dirtier and dirtier.
e They're much happier than they were.
f The cheaper the better.
g The nurse doesn't earn nearly as much as the doctor.
h It's as expensive as them.
i The slower it goes, the safer it is.

B 3
a much/far ... than
b as ... as
c much/far ... than
d much ... than
e as ... as
f a little/a bit ... than
g almost ... as
h not
i worst
j best
k more ... than
l the nicest/the most ordinary/the most normal/the prettiest

C 1
a colder, the coldest
b angrier, the angriest
c more honest, the most honest
d paler, the palest
e better, the best
f more emotional, the most emotional
g kinder, the kindest
h sadder, the saddest
i bluer, the bluest
j faster, the fastest
k more slowly, the most slowly
l better, the best
m more kindly, the most kindly
n worse, the worst
o more often, the most often
p more, the most
q earlier, the earliest
r more frequently, the most frequently

C 2
a more expensive than the brown shoes.
b faster than the tall girl.
c the oldest/eldest.
d the coldest.
e older than the one on the right.
f more dangerous than the road on the left.

C 3
a hotter and hotter
b much more interesting
c a bit more difficult
d the better
e as much as
f as he is
g The bigger
h less than
i the easiest
j and more exciting

C 4
a Brian isn't as tall as his sister.
b Camping holidays are more fun than cruises.
c Flying is more expensive than going by train.
d Heat? The hotter the better.
e In Australia it's hotter in December than in July.
f Last year's holiday was the best one I've ever had.
g Paris is one of the most famous cities in the world.
h She's not as keen on holidays as her sister.
i The roads are getting more and more crowded every year.
j Every year we get a bit wiser.

UNIT 5

A 2
a explanation 2
b explanation 4
c explanation 3
d explanation 2
e explanation 4

A 3
a has lived ... for
b has been ... since
c has worked ... since
d haven't eaten ... for
e has spoken ... since
f 've been ... for
g haven't seen ... since
h 's had ... since

A 4
a Has he finished his meal?
b Has he paid his bill?
c Has he seen/hailed a taxi?
d Has he dropped his wallet?
e Has he lost all his money/Has he got any money?
f Has he given the taxi driver his watch?/Has the taxi driver taken his watch?

B 2
a The boys have been swimming.
b Mark has been cleaning the window.
c It's/It has been snowing.
d Tom has been dancing.
e Jane has been cooking.
f Mr and Mrs Thomas have been shopping.
g Megan has been painting.
h My dog has been digging./My dog has been hiding a bone.

B 3
a She has been learning Greek for three years.
b I've been watching TV since six o'clock.
c John has just been driving his new car.
d I've been living on a houseboat for six months.
e Jane hasn't just been skating on the ice.
f The Gordon family have been going to Ireland every year for ten years.
g Maria has been listening to classical music since she was a child.
h Keith has just been digging a new flower bed.
i Phillip has been working in the City of London since 18 January.
j Susan and Jack have been talking about their relationship for three hours.

B 4
a How long have they been living in America?
b How long have they been living in the beach house?
c How long has Rita been working for Halcyon Music?
d How long has Tom been playing the guitar?
e How long has Rita been studying Japanese?
f How long has Tom been playing with Moondance?

C 1
a 1 have lived 2 have liked 3 have been 4 haven't been able to 5 have never wanted
b 1 have always wanted 2 have been living 3 have been looking
c 1 has driven 2 has repaired 3 has had to 4 has kept 5 has not driven
d 1 have been fishing 2 've caught 3 have you been fishing 4 I've just got back 5 have tried 6 've never been

C 2
a ever tried
b haven't
c haven't done
d ever been
e used
f noticed
g n't had
h been working
i have found
j lost

C 3
a for
b already
c already
d yet
e for
f since
g always
h again
i so
j since

C 4
a How long has Grace been at college?
b How many friends has Grace made?
c Has she joined the drama society?
d Has she managed to get a part in a play?
e How long has Ursula been studying at the college?
f How long have Ursula and Grace been sharing a room?
g Has Grace always been a good student?

h Has she worked hard all/again this term?
i Does Ursula work very hard?
j Has Ursula been working hard since she failed her exams?

UNIT 6

A 2

was built, was constructed, was called, was made, had not ... been invented, were pulled, was designed, were left, is not known, were used, were placed, have been found, is thought, were designed, are visited

A 3

a was built
b was designed
c was thought
d was not given
e was damaged
f were drowned
g were passed
h was established
i was located
j was explored
k have been made
l was released

A 4

a The boy has been hit by the ball
b The house was built in 1886.
c The man has been/is being arrested.
d She has been given an Oscar.
e The biscuits have (all) been eaten.
f The orange has been spilt.

B 2

a was ... known, was called, was published, are inherited – explanation 2
b was known, were built, is used – explanation 3
c are worn, must be washed, should ... be worn – explanation 4
d is burnt, was patented, to be used – explanation 2
e was won, was given, was presented, was awarded – explanation 6

B 3

a 1 A huge cake was baked for the President's daughter by the chef.
2 The President's daughter was baked a huge cake by the chef.
b 1 The new sculpture was shown to the journalists by the director of the gallery.
2 The journalists were shown the new sculpture by the director of the gallery.
c 1 Robbie Williams was offered a multi-million-dollar contract recently.
2 A multi-million-dollar contract was offered to Robbie Williams recently.
d 1 Some war veterans were granted a pardon by the government.
2 A pardon was granted to some war veterans by the government.

C 1

a The picture has been changed.
b A rug has been put on the floor.
c The ornaments have been thrown away.
d A large plant has been put in the fireplace.
e The telephone has been attached to the wall.
f The armchairs and sofa have been taken away.
g The carpet has been taken away.
h Blinds have been installed.
i The walls have been painted white.
j The lampshade has been replaced.

C 2

a was educated
b entered
c was imprisoned
d was not released
e was knighted
f was made/was appointed
g was appointed/was made
h started
i didn't agree
j resigned
k change
l was summoned
m was convicted
n was beheaded
o was made
p died
q is also known
r was written

C 3

a Millions of emails are sent around the world every day.
b The *Mona Lisa* is photographed by a few people every day.
c *Cats*, the musical, has been seen by more people than any other musical.
d Heathrow Airport is used by more than 1.5 million people every year.
e The mountain, Machu Picchu has been visited by 68,000 people since last January.
f Mount Everest is climbed every year by teams from all over the world.
g The 'Vendée Globe' round-the-world yacht race has never been won by a woman.
h The Great Wall of China has been seen by astronauts in space.

UNIT 7

A 2

a present
b future
c past
d future
e present
f present
g future
h future
i future
j future
k present
l past

m future
n future
o future
p future
q future

A 3

a does the show start
b goes up
c is meeting ... doesn't leave
d 're sending
e Are they faxing ... is it coming
f is coming .... is bringing
g are you going
h 'm having
i get .... 'm going
j are you going
k leaves .... don't get
l are leaving

A 4

a Where are you going this afternoon?
b What are you doing this evening?
c When does the film start?
d How is Kevin getting to the station?
e What is on TV this evening?
f Is Jane coming to see us with the new baby?
g When are you going to the supermarket?
h When does the meteorite pass close to the earth?
i How is he getting in touch with you?
j Are you putting sugar in that?

B 2

a is going to buy a newspaper.
b is going to get into a taxi.
c are going to see a film.
d is going to take a photograph.
e is going to climb a tree.
f is going to play his/the guitar.
g going to arrest the thief.
h is going to steal a/the wallet.
i is going to rain.

B 3

a ~~Shall ... try~~ – Is ... going to
b (correct)
c ~~Let~~ – Will
d ~~is going to~~ – will
e (correct)
f ~~will have~~ – is having/is going to have
g ~~'m going to~~ – 'll
h (correct)

B 4

a O
b P
c R
d O
e P
f O
g R
h P
i O
j R
k P

C 1

a are going to – explanation B 2
b 'm going to – explanation B 1
c 're meeting – explanation A 2
d 'll visit – explanation B 3
e is going to – explanation B 1
f 'll make – explanation B 5
g closes – explanation A 1
h 's going to – explanation B 2
i Why don't you – explanation B 6
j Shall I phone – explanation B 7
k 'll miss – explanation B 4
l 'll leave – explanation B 3
m 'll ... see – explanation B 3

C 2

a It's probably going to snow.
b I'm going to the hairdresser tomorrow.
c He's going to faint.
d ... the boat will turn over.
e ... let's have a sandwich.
f The course starts in October.
g Frank is definitely going to win.

h I'll buy you a watch for your birthday!
i Will you pass them to me, please?

C 3
a Are we going to be
b does the train arrive
c isn't getting in
d shall we do/are we going to do
e 'm going to get
f 'll come
g are you going to say/will you say
h 'll do
i 'll just stand
j 'm not going to shout/won't shout
k is he going to do
l 'll probably go
m Are you going to miss/Will you miss
n is going to feel
o closes
p 'll wait
q 'll be

UNIT 8

A 2
a needs to get – explanation 4
b ought to lose – explanation 7
c should improve – explanation 7
d has to go – explanation 4
e mustn't let – explanation 5
f has to drink – explanation 4
g doesn't have to buy – explanation 6
h mustn't wear – explanation 5
i should ... have – explanation 7
j needn't cut out – explanation 6
k must eat – explanation 4
l shouldn't let – explanation 8
m shouldn't spend – explanation 8
n doesn't have to give – explanation 6

A 3
a have to
b have to
c needn't
d shouldn't
e don't have to
f ought not to
g don't have to
h doesn't need to

A 4
a Must I eat my sandwich outside?
b Should I get here before 7 o'clock?
c Do you need to have identification to take books out of the library?
d You needn't worry about the washing up.
e They should hurry up, the concert starts in ten minutes.
f Does she have to take the science exam?
g They had better not spray-paint any more walls.
h Do we need to wear smart clothes for your party?

B 2
a explanation 4
b explanation 3
c explanation 4
d explanation 1
e explanation 5
f explanation 3
g explanation 8
h explanation 3
i explanation 2
j explanation 3
k explanation 7
l explanation 2
m explanation 5
n explanation 2

B 3
a might/may
b can
c may
d could
e can't
f can't

C 1
a should
b should/ought to
c shouldn't
d don't have/don't need
e can't
f can't
g can/could
h could/can
i must/have to
j mustn't/shouldn't
k don't have to
l should/ought to

C 2
a You don't have to get up early tomorrow.
b You don't have to wear a uniform at this school.
c You can't drive along this road.
d You have to wear a uniform in this job.
e You have to retire at 65 in some companies.
f You should go and see a doctor.
g You must tell me if you are going to be late.

C 3
a Harry may/might be going to Chicago
b he can buy a ticket
c He may/might go
d Can I
e You can/may
f can/could you ask me
g I can find
h can work
i it may be
j Can I buy
k You can
l he can have
m might be
n he may/might not be able to

C 4
a You must leave (your) coats and umbrellas at the entrance.
b You must not eat (anything) in the library.
c You must not drink (anything) in the library.
d You must be silent at all times.
e You have to/must wear decent clothes./Your clothes must be decent.
f You don't have to ask before you take a book from the shelves.
g You must replace all your books when you've finished with them.
h You must not/can't take any books out of the library.
i You can use the catalogues.
j You can photocopy documents free.

UNIT 9

A 2
a the man in the blue uniform
b membership card
c sports bag
d anyone without a card
e valuable equipment
f dangerous criminal
g temporary card
h the girl at the desk
i a door at the side of the building
j horrible thing

A 3
a rose ... behind
b red ... in
c tall ... under
d big/red ... in
e old ... on
f black ... behind
g the little/small ... at
h old ... with
i small/short ... beside/by/with
j white ... under/underneath

A 4
a 6
b 9
c 4
d 3
e 2
f 7
g 10
h 11
i 5
j 8
k 1

B 2
a leaning
b taken
c holding
d owned
e sitting
f given
g getting

B 3
a 1 published in the Daily Herald
2 constructed by Cox and Proscutin
3 walking across it
4 employed by the City Council
5 experienced by the public
b 1 driving along the motorway
2 covered in ribbons and sequins
3 brought from Manchester
4 opened by the mayor this morning
c 1 trained in surveillance
2 seen on a security video
3 speaking on television yesterday
4 seeing the criminals

B 4
a trained
b taught
c opening
d created
e produced
f found
g hurrying
h covered
i flowing
j sitting

C 1
a lovely
b last
c old, from number 27
d cooked by his eldest son
e elegant
f blue, covered with expensive paintings
g expensive
h front
i from number 29
j old, green
k two, wearing masks
l with two long barrels
m two long
n biggest, in the house
o large
p parked in front of the house
q two young
r local
s long and detailed
t tall, with the big moustache

C 2
a I like pictures of people with interesting faces.
b Steve has three expensive suits designed by Armani.
c I used to live in a large apartment in the centre of town.
d When you are driving in the snow, you have to be careful of cars skidding on the ice.
e In London tourists often take photographs of soldiers wearing red uniforms and black 'busby' hats.
f I've just bought a first edition of a book written by Steve McCormack.

C 3
a 3
b 1
c 6
d 7
e 8
f 2
g 10
h 9
i 5
j 4

C 4
a The house stands in a road bordered by trees. (The past participle should go after the noun.)
b A very small, yellow bird flew in through the window. (The adjective should go before the noun.)
c I was amazed to see that the man waving at me was my father. (The present participle should go after the noun.)
d *Star Wars* was made by an enormous team of creative people. (The adjective should go before the noun.)
e You should never shout at children behaving badly. (The present participle should go after the noun.)
f I like my garlic bread dripping with butter. (The describing noun should go before the main noun.)
g Mr Keithley loves all the plays written by Shakespeare. (The past participle phrase should go after the noun.)
h His wife owned a large, old-fashioned Chevrolet. (The adjectives should all go before the noun.)
i I support the team playing in red. (The present participle should go after the noun.)
j Michael had a long pointed nose and short hair. (The adjective should go before the noun.)

UNIT 10

A 2
a who/that
b that/which/who
c that/which
d where
e when
f that/which
g who/that
h where
i which/that
j whose

A 3
a ✓
b ✗ who/that
c ✗ who/that
d ✓
e ✗ which/that
f ✓
g ✗ who/that
h ✗ which/that

A 4
a who had once been his girlfriend
b that she had given him all those years ago
c who served him
d which meant that no one had to fill in tickets any more
e that is electronically sensitive
f that he had ever seen
g who invented this stupid machine
h that he thought she would hate

B 2
a This is Catherine, who I met on holiday last year.
b Keith bought this guitar, which was once played by Eric Clapton.
c That's Robert, who is getting married next week.
d We had lunch in town, in the new restaurant which was opened by David Beckham.
e That's my friend Mark, who I often play tennis with.
f This girl is Laurie, who's going to live in Australia.

g We had a lovely time at the party, when all the family was together.

B 3
a who is Jake's brother
b who is his/Jake's other brother
c which was very cheap
d which was a very new type of computer
e who was his neighbour
f who was Geraldine's dog
g who was his doctor
h who was another doctor
i who was his other neighbour
j who was Gloria's dog
k who was another doctor
l where Jake wanted to live

C 1
a that/which
b who/that
c who
d which/that
e whose
f whose
g which/ that
h who/which/that
i who
j where

C 2
a
b who/that
c
d that/which
e who
f who
g
h who
i
j which/that
k who
l whose
m
n who

C 3
a Drivers who drive too slowly are really annoying.
b He wanted to wear the jacket that his wife had given him.
c I can still remember the day when you got back from university.
d I don't like people who smoke all the time.
e The kind of soup that I like is hot and freshly made.
f Last week I met someone who I hadn't seen for months.
g The kind of music that Steve likes is the kind of music I just can't bear.
h She will never forget that moment when they announced the winner.
i The book that I was reading when you saw me was very interesting.
j That's the director of *The Multitude*, whose latest film made a million dollars.

UNIT 11

A 2
a must have – explanation 8
b could have – explanation 3
c couldn't – explanation 5
d could have – explanation 3
e might have – explanation 1
f can't have – explanation 9
g couldn't – explanation 7
h may have – explanation 1
i might not have – explanation 2

A 3
a 7
b 5
c 2
d 4
e 8
f 3
g 6
h 1

A 4

a Picasso could/might have painted this picture.
b He can't have painted it in just two hours.
c She must have been rich.
d They might have taken the painting during the night.

B 2

a had to – explanation 1
b didn't need to – explanation 5
c should have – explanation 3
d didn't have to – explanation 2
e had to – explanation 1
f had to – explanation 1
g shouldn't have – explanation 4
h didn't have to – explanation 2

B 3

a had to
b didn't have to
c had to
d didn't need to
e should have
f had to
g had to
h shouldn't have
i had to
j needed to/had to
k should have
l didn't have to
m didn't need to
n had to

C 1

a You must have thought
b Somebody must have
c Someone else couldn't have
d Someone who works for the airline might have
e Someone who works here couldn't have
f Someone might have
g It might have been

C 2

a must
b couldn't
c might
d can't
e might
f shouldn't
g couldn't
h must
i had to
j can't
k might
l couldn't
m should

UNIT 12

A 2

a I'll go to the shop.
b I'll buy a lottery ticket.
c If I buy a lottery ticket, I'll watch the lottery programme on TV this evening.
d If I watch the lottery programme on TV this evening, I'll be disappointed.
e I'll buy a boat.
f If I buy a boat, I'll sail to the USA.
g If I sail to the USA, I'll visit Las Vegas.
h If I visit Las Vegas, I'll lose all my money.

A 3

a 4
b 6
c 7
d 3
e 1
f 5
g 2

B 2

a would
b would
c were
d have
e have
f would
g hadn't
h would
i didn't
j 'd
k were

B 3

a If I changed my job I would be a teacher.
b If I had been listening to the radio I would have heard about the traffic jams on the motorway.
c If I were a gardener I would spend all my time outdoors.
d If I won the lottery I would buy a new house.

C 1

a were ... would give
b would be ... came
c were ... wouldn't say
d say ... will get
e win ... will be
f doesn't start ... will be/'s going to be
g were not ... would still be
h were ... would stop

C 2

a 2
b 2
c 1
d 1
e 1
f 2
g 2

C 3

a been
b had
c If
d wanted
e wouldn't
f fallen
g hadn't
h fused
i lit
j had
k will

UNIT 13

A 2

a 2
b 1
c 1
d 2
e 2
f 1
g 1

A 3

a to go
b going
c to go
d to get
e seeing
f to play
g to win
h playing
i going
j to turn
k going
l being
m being
n to let
o to go

A 4

a appear to have
b agreed to let
c offered to pay
d wanted to do
e imagined starring
f failed to become
g enjoyed doing
h admit to being
i managed to get
j plan to stop
k hope to go
l want to be
m miss working
n promised to keep
o dislike saying
p tend to prefer

B 2

Example answers

a She stopped what she was doing and tied her shoelaces.
b She remembered that she had met him at a concert.
c Keith forgot that he had sent that letter to his friend.
d I was running and stopped to rest.
e I hope you will remember that you must/should phone me.
f She has not watered the plants because she forgot.
g We talk all the time.

B 3

a that she had
b (that) she had taken
c offering/to offer
d talking
e taking/to take
f crying/to cry
g listening/ to listen
h being/to be
i asking
j crying
k (that) he believed
l (that) he was (being)
m (that) Ruth should watch
n (that) she would do

C 1

a I enjoy playing tennis.
b I expect to finish the job in a couple of hours.
c Phil denied borrowing her bicycle.
d Phil offered to mend it.
e Phil agreed to buy a new bell.
f I avoided doing any work yesterday.
g I remember playing tennis with my cousin when I was young.

h I want to go to Italy this summer.
i Phil suggested buying a new computer.
j I decided to do it.
k My cousin forgot to (come to) play tennis with me.

C 2

a skydiving
b skydiving/to skydive
c skydiving
d to skydive
e to skydive
f skydiving
g to skydive
h to skydive
i skydiving

C 3

a 2
b 6
c 1
d 5
e 10
f 7
g 9
h 4
i 3
j 11
k 8

C 4

a Mary agreed that she would go skating.
b Ann forgot that she had to phone her boss.
c Tom promised that he would help with the house move.
d Jo denied that she had eaten Graham's sandwiches.
e Graham promised that he would forget about it.
f Sue remembered that she had eaten the cake.
g Arthur agreed that he had behaved badly.

UNIT 14

A 2

a Mary said she had lived there for two years.
b Peter said he studied music.
c Paul and Kenny said they worked in a software company.
d Mrs Yamanachi said she would finish her course in six months.
e Ellen said she would graduate next year.
f Matt said he was going to join a rock band.
g Sally said her brother was going to work in a law firm in London.
h Kate and Jane said they had just watched a football match on TV.
i Simon said he had just been to New York for the first time.
j Anita said she was going to marry George.
k Henry said he would be there in a minute.

A 3

a had met
b had fallen
c had never been
d had to go
e could not
f would
g had not/has not
h missed/misses
i We met on holiday last year.
j We fell in love almost at once.
k I had never been in love before.
l I have to go home in two days.
m I cannot stay for another week.
n I'll see you in three weeks.
o I haven't seen her since that day.
p I still miss her.

B 2

a had
b him
c taken it out
d would be
e couldn't
f advised
g agreed
h that
i be able to
j was
k what
l told

B 3

a asked if I
b wondered if we were/would be late
c who she was
d wondered whether to go
e thought they would do
f (correct)
g (correct)
h invited Mark to see
i tell Tom to buy

B 4

a invited
b said
c ordered
d promised
e persuade
f asked
g advised
h want

C 1

a I asked Bob if he was coming round that night.
b He said he was going to meet his mates at the skateboard park.
c I asked him if he wanted to come round later.
d He said no thanks, he thought it would be too late.
e I asked him if he wanted to go to the ballet with me next week.
f He said he didn't think he wanted to see me again.
g I asked him if I was too boring.
h He said no, of course not. It was just that he preferred girls who like/liked skateboarding better than ballet.

C 2

a Inspector Portwood wants to know if you can see them.
b She says she can see them now.
c He wants to know what they are doing now.
d She says they are sitting on a park bench.
e He wants to know if they are talking to each other.
f She says she thinks they are talking.
g He wants to know if they have got anything in their hands.
h She says she's passing him a small package.
i He wants to know what's in the package.
j She says it's just sandwiches!